LEARNING RUSSIAN MARATHON:

How to speak Russian in 10 years

Effective strategies to improve your Russian,
solutions to the most common difficulties and
video bonuses to put all of this into practice

Denis P. Ivanov

D1699194

LEARNING RUSSIAN MARATHON:
How to speak Russian in 10 years

For more information contact www.learningrussianmarathonbook.com

First Edition: October 2015

10 9 8 7 6 5 4 3 2 1

Preface

Reading this book won't make you magically start speaking Russian, and that's not what it's for. 60 pages wouldn't be enough for this and, well, neither would 1,000. But I'm more than sure you'll find something useful here!

I've got enough experience to boldly state that around 90% of Russian learners never achieve the result they're after. Just think about that for a second – 90%! Sadly, any honest, professional teacher will tell you the same.

As a rough estimate, learning Russian can take over 1,000 hours. That is a serious investment of time. Before opening up that huge grammar book and diving into endless audio courses, stop and ask yourself: how can I achieve my goal as quickly as possible? How can I avoid wasting my time?

Effective! You'll spend a few hours reading this book and end up saving so much more time on learning Russian. You'll know for sure that you don't need to waste money and time. I created this book to be the most effective time investment you can possibly make.

Practical! Based on years of experience, I've collected the most common problems learners encounter. There is a solution to each and every one of these problems – a method that will rescue any struggling Russian learner.

Easy! All the skills and methods that I will teach you can be put into action right away, without any previous practise. In fact, you often won't even need a teacher. And don't forget to collect your bonuses; they'll kick-start the learning process.

You can be an amazing Russian speaker. I'll teach you how.

Denis P. Ivanov
Dedicated to all those who teach and learn Russian, the veterans and the beginners.

Contents

Why pronunciation is more than just aesthetic, and a look at speech positions. Learn the best way to pronounce Russian properly at normal speed. Bonus Repetition lesson!

Why are we so afraid of speaking Russian? Where does this stress come from? Get ready to try the most effective, stress-free way of speaking fluent Russian. Bonus Storytelling video!

Is Russian speech really that fast? Why is it so hard for us to understand? Find the source of listening comprehension problems and try out a simple solution.

Introduction

According to legend, there once lived a Greek warrior by the name of Pheidippides. He is said to have run from Marathon to Athens to deliver news of a military victory against the Persians in the Battle of Marathon. When he reached Athens, he proclaimed, *"Rejoice, we conquer!"* and dropped dead. You probably understand what I'm inferring here – for many people, learning Russian is like running a marathon.

My years of experience have shown me that most Russian learners feel like marathon runners: then run nonstop, apply huge effort to learning, spend money on materials – and the finish line is nowhere to be seen.

But here you are, ready to read this book. What are your expectations? To learn the 'secret sauce' to master Russian? To discover the most cutting-edge, latest approach? Native fluency in just one week?

Let me be completely honest with you

I would never say that you can't learn Russian without my help or advice. Look at the 250 million Russian speakers – they all somehow managed it without my help.

I haven't invented any super-secret techniques for learning Russian, not by a long shot. But what *I do* is give you the most proven and effective approaches to learning Russian to fluency. All the methods follow a logical progression and are illustrated with practical examples. To make things even clearer, I've added in some video lessons that you can try right away to apply what you've learned.

I'm hesitant to say that you will achieve miraculous results, but the human brain *is* capable of incredible things when it is applied properly.

So how can this book help?

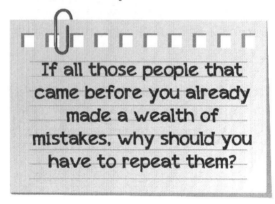

If all those people that came before you already made a wealth of mistakes, why should you have to repeat them?

Just think how many people have learned Russian before you – probably millions! They hit problems, stopped and started and didn't give up. If all those people that came before you already made a wealth of mistakes, why should you have to repeat them? Wouldn't it be better to tap into those years of experience and declare: *"Guys, here are tens of problems that Russian learners have,"* and *"Here is the best and most effective solution to these problems."*

Well, I think we can do just that!

This is what I am doing with this book. For every problem, I have a solution and corresponding method. These methods are clear and simple to apply, but highly effective.

Maybe you can make it without my advice

It will probably take you a few hours to read through this book, depending on how quickly you read in English. It will also take about an hour to watch all the bonuses that come with the book – www.learningrussianmarathonbook.com (they include demo lessons that help you put what you've learned into practise).

Perhaps a handful of readers might even save some time by skipping this altogether. For those select few, I recommend that you come back and read this book another time.

You should **stop** reading this book right now if you:

- Have zero problems or issues learning Russian (problems like a small vocabulary, grammar difficulties, or understanding spoken Russian).

- Know how to develop all the necessary language skills in the most optimal fashion.

- Are an experienced language learner and already have your own proven system for learning new languages (although I'm sure that experienced learners will love my book too).

- Don't want to change anything in your approach and are 100% happy with your progress.

If that is the case, I am genuinely happy for you, happy that you are moving forward. Put this book aside and come back to it later when you feel you need it, when you need some new ideas, answers, or effective technical approaches. I welcome with open arms any student who wants to better themselves and become smarter.

Don't even think about learning Russian!

There was a time, many years ago, when I met a Russian learner for the first time. It was all the way across the globe in Australia.

I was amazed that anyone would even think to study Russian.

"How long have you been studying Russian?" I asked.

With a thick accent he answered in Russian, *"Tee...ten years."*

He stuttered, mixed up his words and could barely get a phrase out. And that was the result of ten years of study!

And this got me thinking: humans have achieved extraordinary things – we can travel across the globe in a day, deliver messages in fractions of a second, send robots to Mars and so much more. And yet, when we want to learn a language quickly, we get bombarded with 100 different approaches. And what result do we get?

Russian language students (and students of other languages too) are still running marathons to Athens, and most of them end up dropping dead (figuratively, of course). So why can't we just hop in a car and drive to Athens in 30 minutes?

As you may have noticed, the language learning industry puts out a huge number of products. But has learning a language become any quicker or easier?

No, but it has become more expensive! I firmly believe that this industry has zero incentive to make life easier for the student. Every year we see more and more new apps, systems and courses. Does that mean the old ones were 'wrong'? Today, students can easily build themselves a library of materials and systems, but do they teach the language any faster than the materials that were available 100 years ago?

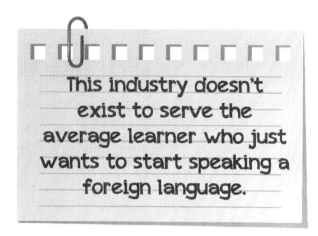

This industry doesn't exist to serve the average learner who just wants to start speaking a foreign language.

I can say with a great deal of certainty that there is plenty of room for improvement. The teaching industry that sells you books and lessons has no intention of solving your problems. This industry doesn't exist to serve the average learner who just wants to start speaking a foreign language. What it does do is separate you from your cash.

So please don't harbour any illusions that some 'professional' will actually insert knowledge directly into your brain. You have to read, break down and understand what you are doing and why!

Everything I know about learning languages

I often have to explain the pitfalls of language learning, explain the right way to do things and prove things. And what's the most common answer I hear in response to my explanations? *"I wish I had known this years ago, I would have saved a ton of time."*

You see, there was a time not so long ago that I was in the same desperate situation, stuck in a dead end and far away from the results I wanted.

Now things are different, and every day I become more convinced that we can drastically change the approach to learning Russian and make it more effective. It's just a matter of setting the right course and explaining what exactly needs to be done and why. I thought it was a shame that there was no way to work with lots of students at once, to make sure everyone could see that *there is a better way*. It was this thought that led me to write this book and create this course!

I have put everything I know about learning Russian in this book.

In the coming pages I will share with you some stories of people that I have worked with over the past years. You will learn from these examples and become familiar with some of my favourite approaches. We will look at the simplest cases and the most seemingly impossible.

I wrote this book for you and for me. My son speaks Russian and English and is now mastering Chinese. I need to keep up. When I'm in 'teaching mode' everything is fine, but when I am in learner mode, I myself sometimes need to take a minute and remind myself how I should be doing things.

How to read this book
Every chapter is structured around a solution-based approach. You don't have to read the whole book in order; you can choose your weak area and start with that right away.

In each chapter I introduce you to an unsuccessful student (if you see something in common with them, definitely read that chapter). I break down the reasons for the student's failure and, although there is some theory, I keep things interesting. Then I give you the method and approach to conquer the problem.

My assumptions about you

When I started writing this book, I tried to imagine what my reader was going to be like. In the end, I came up with a list of assumptions about who I think wants to read this book. I hope you recognize yourself in these descriptions!

- You want to learn or are learning Russian but you still aren't fluent.

- You are prepared to spend a few hours reading this book to save yourself a lot of time and effort in the long run.

- You don't expect to magically start speaking Russian once you finish this book.

- And most of all, you are not satisfied with your results in learning Russian!

Where to go from here

Head over to the next section: *"Reprogramming yourself to become a successful learner"*. Over a couple of pages I explain the fundamentals of language learning. Also check out the *"We didn't know the formula"* section. This is a condensed description of the shortest path to achieving your goal, step by step. You'll get a bird's eye view of the whole process.

If you like, you can skip the problem description and jump straight into the solution. Take a look at the *"Chapter 7: Practical steps – act right now"*. There you'll be able to read about these new approaches and put them into practise too.

Reprogramming yourself to become a successful learner

I didn't write this book to show you quick tricks to learning a language and then try and upsell you some other product with yet more bells and whistles. Not at all. My mission goes a lot further than that.

I'm almost sure that the approach you are using now is not giving you the results you need or want; otherwise, why would you be reading this book? I want to change your approach to learning languages in general, not just Russian. I want to change it fundamentally and to the core.

To achieve a change
like this you might
imagine you'd need a
huge book, maybe even
a small library.

To achieve a change like this you might imagine you'd need a huge book, maybe even a small library. And still, some people might never be convinced, not with all the books in the world. So, to avoid writing massive, long volumes, I will be as concise and convincing as possible.

Allow me to introduce you to the 7 fundamentals of language learning.

They make up the foundation of everything I describe in this book.

Far before our time, Aristotle and Euclid made use of fundamental principles too, not for the Russian language, of course, but for mathematics. If we hadn't accepted these fundamentals of mathematics, we would all still be stuck at the level of ancient Greece – we would have made no progress.

In much the same way, I want you to become familiar with these 7 language learning fundamentals. This will be a huge step forward for you. It will 'reprogram' you and change the way you think about language learning. You'll be on a new, shorter and more effective path toward your goal.

So, with that in mind, here are the 7 fundamentals…

Fundamental 1: Fluency and speed are more important than 'complexity'

In real life, there is no slow version of the Russian language. Even children speak almost as fast as adults. But there is a difference in the level of complexity of language, from simple answers to complex structures. Learning a language in its natural form should always be a priority for everyone, children and adults alike. You should speak *fluently* at a simple level first and only then move on to more complex language, academic forms etc. Language learning at any level should be as close to natural speed as possible.

Fundamental 2: Real language doesn't require any artificial written forms

Russian is only written in Cyrillic. In the real world, that is the only way you'll see Russian. All the different varieties of transliteration are artificial creations that are only of use in very limited situations. To speak fluently, you don't need transliteration and, in fact, it does more harm than good.

Fundamental 3: Spoken language is more important than written language, and listening comes before reading

For any living language, speaking comes first and writing comes later on. That's the way a child starts learning. In real life, written language is only a priority in some limited situations (for example if a person has hearing problems). Learning a language *isn't a limited situation*, which is why we make speaking and listening our priorities. Writing comes as an addition; it's still important, but speaking is the priority.

Fundamental 4: Grammar rules don't develop language skills

Grammar rules represent a theoretical language model – an artificial creation. This model gives us grammar knowledge that can't always be used in live speech. Skills are what we use, not grammar rules. If our skills are honed, then we don't need to know all the rules and exceptions in order to speak correctly. We don't ask, *"Why do they say it like this or that?"* Learning grammar can help us organise the knowledge that *we already have*, but it is impossible to develop the skill of fluency by just learning grammar rules.

Fundamental 5: When speaking, we use language chunks

We don't speak in separate words, sounds, syllables, or sentences, and especially not paragraphs. Our speech is made up of groups of words that usually come together in language chunks. I don't mean like proverbs, but rather set phrases. It's precisely these chunks (not words) that people use to express meaning. Good knowledge of these chunks is what makes our speech fluent and natural, just like a native speaker. Remember, in written language, words are just building blocks; they're not ready for use on their own.

Fundamental 6: Conversation is not a natural source of stress and tension

Learning a language and using it is a skill that we all have. It's a just a part of daily life, no different from walking or eating. Like with those basic skills, language learning shouldn't be a cause of stress. If you got stressed out from talking a walk, that would be abnormal. Stress when speaking is equally abnormal. The argument that 'stress is normal to start with' is unfounded; after all, we all learn to speak our native tongue with no stress at all. It's more likely that a negative reaction is caused by the situation, not from speaking. You should avoid these types of situations – repeated exposure to this kind of stress will stunt your progress and you'll lose your motivation.

Fundamental 7: Flawless grammar is unnecessary and impossible to achieve

The language of communication is a very practical tool. Pronunciation, vocabulary and grammar are used freely by native speakers and can be consciously changed at a whim. The most outstanding native speakers (poets, writers etc.) continuously create new words and new turns of phrase.

Unlike in computer languages, in human languages we can make mistakes and have discrepancies. We can go as far as to say that there is no absolute standard – that's why it's nothing out of the ordinary to make mistakes, no matter if you are a native or a language learner. You can of course shoot for 100% grammatical accuracy, but I believe that it is both impossible and not what you should be aiming for. The real goal is an exchange of information.

****

So why do I refer to these as fundamentals, and why do I suggest you accept them without question?

Because I want to save you time. Proving the obvious wastes a lot of time.

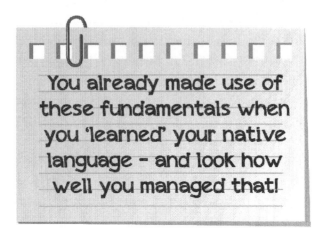

You already made use of these fundamentals when you 'learned' your native language – and look how well you managed that!

You already made use of these fundamentals when you 'learned' your native language – and look how well you managed that!

Keep reading this book and you will see me return to these fundamentals and explain them further. You will also see for yourself how self-evident all these points really are.

We didn't know the formula

I think it wouldn't be outrageous to claim that the majority of new learners (and even experienced ones) really don't know how to study a language. Quite often we don't know what we need to do to achieve our goal.

We attack the problem 'blindfolded'.

If you ask a learner what exactly he/she needs to start speaking correct, fluent Russian, they probably won't have much of an answer for you! It's strange, because a learner is ready to spend hundreds, if not thousands, of hours studying a language, and yet they don't think about exactly how they will go about doing it.

What should we start with? What skills and in what order? What's the fast way to achieve our goal? Sadly, this is what the answer to this question usually looks like:

"I'll hire a teacher, I saw some cheap ones online, or maybe I'll sign up for a course. I saw a language school near work."

"I have a good grammar book with audio and I just need a good phonetics course, can you recommend one?"

"Someone recommended a great computer program, I'll download it. It has some really good audio courses."

Do you recognise any of these answers? That's the way all our example students from this book thought. We *all* thought that learning a language is basically a system of textbooks, courses and teachers.

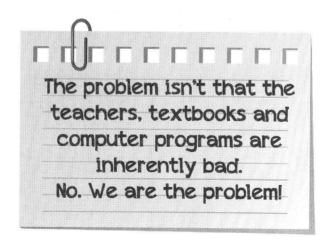

The problem isn't that the teachers, textbooks and computer programs are inherently bad.
No. We are the problem!

The problem isn't that the teachers, textbooks and computer programs are inherently bad. No. We are the problem!

We think that someone has already thought out how to do it for us.

If someone calls himself a Russian teacher and charges 50 (or 5) dollars for a lesson, he/she probably knows how to teach you Russian, correct? Do authors of mass-published text books know best how to teach you Russian? If you find a new computer program with a nice interface, does that mean the author has implemented the most cutting-edge learning techniques?

If we think that someone else has thought it all out for us, we'll end up with complaints. Complaints about: our 'lack of linguistic ability', 'how hard Russian is', 'bad memory' and so on.

Don't rely on anyone else.

The language learning formula: 7 simple steps

Bad news. The most common reason for failing to learn Russian is a long, unnatural, ineffective approach. What's worse, you're probably already using this approach. But the good news is that you don't need a university degree in linguistics in order to choose the right approach. **It's simple!**

You don't need professors creating specially designed plans for you. **This approach is universal!**

Really, learning a language is a fairly common process, like just learning to walk. The difference is that, when you learned your native language, you didn't think about how you would do it. You had one approach – a natural, simple and effective approach.

Now you're all grown up and have forgotten how to study a language. You have the choice of hundreds of methods and thousands of textbooks. But as you know, it's easy to get lost in the jungle of materials.

But don't despair just yet. We can still find the simplest and most effective path to learning Russian. As usual, we'll start right back at very beginning…

1. Forming the correct speech position

In different languages, even similar sounds can sound completely different. The reason for this is that for Russian native speakers the speech apparatus is in one position and for, say, Chinese, Italian or English speakers – it's in another. That why even the simplest words, like STOP, for example, will sound different when pronounced by Russian and English people. You would think that sounds are sounds in any language. But no, 'similar' sounds are pronounced from differing speech positions, and the difference will be obvious.

Trying to pronounce foreign words without adopting the correct speech position is a common mistake among language learners. Even listening to a language without knowing about phonetics is both hard and counterproductive. **Forming the correct speech positions is the first step in the language learning formula – nothing can come before it**. Even learning the Russian alphabet can be studied at the same time, but not before. After all, what would be the point in learning letters that you can't pronounce properly? Do you want to speak Russian with English pronunciation? I certainly hope not!

Now we have adopted the right speech position, we are ready to practise it and put it to use at the next stage...

2. Pronouncing at a natural speed

If your speech apparatus has never been put to use in Russian speech positions, you need to develop it to do so. You'll need to start slowly, pronouncing sounds, single syllables and then, finally, words.

That's how a child learns. Children can't hold a conversation and can't read, they start pronouncing separate sounds – that's the example you want to follow. By choosing the right exercises, an adult student can master a few skills at once: listening, reading, pronunciation and vocabulary learning.

This is where we 'switch' our vocal apparatus to 'Russian mode'. No more slow speech: what we are aiming for is functional, natural speed – even if it means sacrificing pronunciation quality.

If you skip this step without learning to pronounce out loud at a natural speed, you might as well not bother moving on to any of the other language skills. What's more, this step is extra important to ensure you don't have problems with listening comprehension, which is what I want to talk about next.

3. Keeping up with the flow of speech

At this stage, your vocal apparatus should be familiar with Russian speech, although it might not be fully used to it yet.

We need to completely forget about textbook-speed Russian and move directly to natural speed. That's why the active phase of this step is listening. Your vocal apparatus is still not able to process written Russian into spoken Russian – you'll still be susceptible to making mistakes and 'creating' your own pronunciations. In other words, just reading without audio will probably be more of a hindrance than a help. One important thing to note here is that you need to listen *and pronounce.* All faculties of your vocal apparatus must be working in synch, and they are all interconnected. Keep things this way and don't 'cripple' your vocal apparatus!

Full immersion and a little bit of positive stress can help you move past this stage. If you don't learn to keep up with the flow, you'll fall behind and have more permanent problems with listening comprehension.

4. Building vocabulary

After working through the previous three steps, we're ready to build our vocabulary. The most effective way to build vocabulary will be reading, because that's the easiest way of spotting and noting new words.

You always need to be highlighting language chunks, not separate words. You need to build your vocabulary from grammatically correct, ready-to-use constructs. Use your 'memory blocks' more effectively.

At this stage, you won't be at risk of memorising the wrong pronunciation and you can move on to reading larger volumes of text. But that doesn't mean you need to read in silence. You need you listen and pronounce new words. This is key. After all, you don't just plan on using these words in written form alone!

Only once you complete this step are you ready to move on to grammar!

5. Internalizing grammar forms

All our progress so far has given us enough of a foundation to have an idea about Russian grammar forms. In our heads, we already have some simple language constructs memorised. What is important is being able to use grammar, not just know it. From the audio and texts, you should have a feeling for what sounds correct and what sounds incorrect. But it would be more logical to take things to the next level and continue honing the skills you've already been working on.

In fact, it would be best to increase your study efforts. It means using intensive, multiple variations, use of different grammar forms to express the same ideas and thoughts. You need to 'attack' Russian grammar fearlessly from all possible angles.

And what about the knowledge? Well, theoretical knowledge can help us cement our understanding and perception of Russian grammar, but this consolidation comes last, not first.

And now, being grammatically correct allows us to take things to a higher level, a natural level.

6. Becoming a natural

Being grammatically correct doesn't mean you have a natural feel for the language. A student with fantastic grammar, great pronunciation and a big vocabulary can still sound unnatural when speaking, nothing like a native speaker.

Sounding natural is a separate skill with separate steps to mastery – steps that often get overlooked. All the things you did in the previous steps gave you some of the elements of sounding natural. Now is the time to focus on expressing your thoughts in a natural way, not just in a grammatically correct way.

As usual, we can wait for this to happen 'in its own time', or we can turbocharge it.

24

An effective way of doing this is by making use of written exercises. Doing this is the simplest and most logical way to transform your thoughts into natural expression.

You can theoretically do similar exercises verbally with a native speaker, but doing that brings us close to a touchy subject for many students – the fear of speaking…

Pseudo 7. Holding a conversation!

I call this one 'pseudo 7', and there's a good reason for that. Speaking doesn't come right at the end, it's just that there isn't a fixed position for it in our formula. You perform this step when you feel like it.

You can start speaking at step 2, 5 or even 7. Whenever you feel ready.

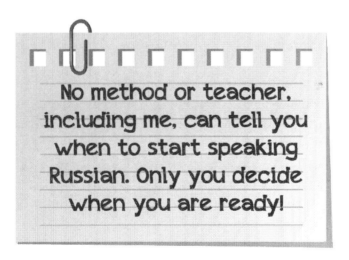

No method or teacher, including me, can tell you when to start speaking Russian. Only you decide when you are ready!

No method or teacher, including me, can tell you when to start speaking Russian. Only you decide when you are ready!

We see a lot of problems when students are forced to speak too early. It's a major cause of language barriers and negative associations with speaking Russian.

The task for both textbooks and teachers alike is to create an environment that lets a student take the first steps to speaking without stress. Sounds like a fairy-tale scenario! But don't worry; there are methods we can use that won't take you right out of your comfort zone!

******

It really is simple.

But here's what usually happens: the unsuccessful student takes the long path, starting with elements from the end or middle of the formula I have laid out. They miss something and bounce back and forth. They learn the alphabet and move straight to grammar. They try to speak, they turn to the dictionary. More grammar. Then they get demotivated…

They might, say, start with step 4. The student has no idea about phonetics and pronunciation and then starts memorizing Russian words. The result? Difficulty actually using learned vocabulary because the student doesn't know how to pronounce things properly. Sooner or later, the student has to come back to the previous step and learn to pronounce the learned words. In other words, he/she is doing twice the work, relearning things, but with correct pronunciation.

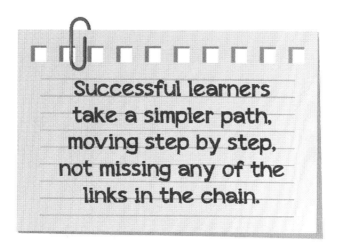

Successful learners take a simpler path, moving step by step, not missing any of the links in the chain.

Successful learners take a simpler path, moving step by step, not missing any of the links in the chain. That's the way native speakers do things, and they are the most successful students of all.

So do as the natives do!

In the coming chapters, we'll take a close-up look at how to perform all these steps in *the right order* and how to avoid doing things in the wrong order.

Chapter 1. Pronunciation can ruin everything

Why pronunciation is more than just aesthetic, and a look at speech positions. Learn the best way to pronounce Russian properly at normal speed. Bonus Repetition lesson!

Who: Pierre, France. Has been studying Russian for 5 years.
The problem: For Pierre, spoken Russian words sound long and unpronounceable.
Notes: Pierre is worried about his pronunciation and is constantly studying articulation. The diagnosis: fear of bad pronunciation.

What the KGB thought about pronunciation

In the Soviet Union of the 1970s the KGB gave instructions on how to detect a spy. One of the first signs was *"incorrect pronunciation of Russian words, especially words that sound similar to foreign words (telegram, telephone), and a lack of regional dialect."*

Other spy signs on the KGB list included a person's dress style, eating habits and other behaviour signs.

The KGB didn't tell people how to catch spies based on incorrect case or conjugation usage.

Well, I think we can agree that it's much easier to learn not to put your feet on the table or not to put ice in your vodka than it is to pronounce 'Broadway' with a Russian accent. What is interesting is that nowhere did the KGB mention anything about incorrect grammar. The KGB didn't tell people how to catch spies based on incorrect case or conjugation usage.

You might be surprised and wonder, *"Out of all the complexities of the Russian language, how come they only focused on pronunciation?!?"* I can't say for sure, but I recommend that you listen to the KGB advice because they sure knew what they were doing!

Pronunciation is a part of human nature. What's more, it's a deeply rooted part of our nature. In fact, it's so deep that we don't even notice the nuances of pronunciation in our own language. So imagine trying to catch them in a foreign language!

Sherlock Holmes could tell exactly which part of England a speaker was from by their accent. In the same way, Professor Higgins, the professor of phonetics in Bernard Shaw's *Pygmalion*, could tell in which region a person lived. It was pronunciation that set d'Artagnan apart from Parisians and told us he was from Gascony.

And hey, musketeers aside, I myself moved from the south of Russia to Moscow and for years pronounced my /g/ like /h/ – which Muscovites really found amusing.

***

After all that KGB talk, you're probably expecting me to teach you some super-secret master spy pronunciation technique. Perhaps you can already see yourself speaking to a Russian native speaker and having them mistake you for a local from Ryazan or the Urals…

But alas, that's just a fantasy!

Instead of 'hunting' for spy techniques, we are going to be setting goals and relentlessly working towards them!

Why you'll probably never sound like a Russian

Let me break the bad news first: you, as a determined adult, will probably never speak Russian and sound like a Russian local. As you may have guessed from the chapter name, it's not because of your vocabulary or verb of motion conjugation – not even the instrumental case. No, it's because of pronunciation!

Jumping ahead a little, I want to tell you that poorly-developed pronunciation can stunt the development of other language skills too. But more on that later.

The first obstacle to perfect pronunciation – your ears.

Here is a sad, but proven scientific fact: during adulthood, we all lose our ability to finely differentiate sounds that are not present in our native languages.

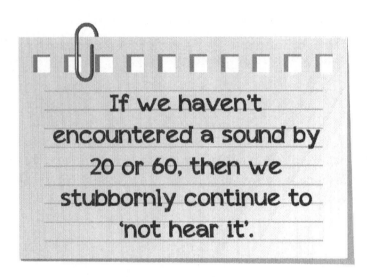

If we haven't encountered a sound by 20 or 60, then we stubbornly continue to 'not hear it'.

If we haven't encountered a sound by 20 or 60, then we stubbornly continue to 'not hear it'.

More specifically, we hear sounds the same way: it's not like our ears get blocked. But to differentiate the sounds the same way a native speaker does is impossible. Sensitivity to 'foreign' sounds will never be the same as with your native language. For example, to a Russian speaker the words 'ship' and 'sheep' sound (and are often pronounced) the same (they are similar, of course). In much the same way, English speakers confuse the 'hard' and 'soft' /L/ sounds in Russian.

Obstacle two – your tongue

The muscles in a native speaker's speech apparatus work in different ways in different languages. Just like when playing different sports, different muscles contract more than others.

And so, at some point in our adult lives, we decide to start speaking a new language, Russian for example. We hear the Russian, check the pronunciation table, learn how to position our tongues and so on. And how's the result? Not so great! The muscles needed for Russian sounds are simply undertrained. They are basically atrophied from years of never being used. And now you need some intensive training to bring them 'back to life' and start pronouncing new sounds with the correct flow.

So it looks like a fairly sad state of affairs with pronunciation. Like we're limping along on one leg... We can barely hear new Russian words and we confuse them all the time. And let's not forget that we can't pronounce anything properly because the speech muscles we have don't work. Speaking is like trying to say something after waking up from anaesthesia.

Here's a fact: a very small percentage of adults can quickly (think a few years) learn and master a foreign language's pronunciation like a native speaker and *sound like* a native speaker. The rest of us still speak with an accent, even after years and years of being immersed in the culture. Even in the most fluent, a tiny, barely noticeable accent will usually still remain.

If you don't have a genetic gift for languages, do you have a chance at great success with Russian? Yes you do, I'm sure of it.

So this is where I would like us to get a little philosophical.

Language and self-identity

I am deeply convinced that a language is not some technical instrument for sorting through information flows. You make grammar and phonetics mistakes – language flow is poor; you improve grammar and phonetics – language flow is optimal. I feel that is a very utilitarian and limited way of thinking about the role of language.

Language is more likely part of a person's nature, like habits and mannerisms. That is why, to learn like a native, you firstly need to **conquer the purely linguistic barrier**. So learn to pronounce properly, train your speech apparatus and so on.

And secondly, the hardest part, **conquer the psychological barrier**. Allow me to explain. What happens when we speak a foreign language, including Russian? Excluding school learning where we sit behind our desks and learn, what happens is **we take on a new role**. We change the way we speak and gesticulate, our facial expressions change and the way we think changes too. In other words, we change our self-identity! I dare say that, without this change in self-identity, it will never be possible to speak at a native level.

I don't know whether these observations will sound good or scary to you (*"Oh no, I don't want to act like a Russian!"*), but in this chapter, we will be focusing mostly on the linguistic aspects of pronunciation.

Want to be a spy?

We've spent a few pages talking about the hard road to pronunciation, and I've given you some scary facts too. So, now it's time for us to really understand: what is our real goal when working on pronunciation? We know that pronunciation is important and that we need it, but just what kind of results can we actually achieve?

Here I would like to offer you two options.

Option one is what I call 'the spy with no accent'.

The goal in this case is to have pronunciation like a native speaker, to sound just like a native. This is one of the hardest possible goals, but, strangely enough, most learners, at least subconsciously, want to achieve this.

OK, great! That level of Russian is only necessary for someone who needs to blend in completely with the culture. For spies – my favourite example. I find it hard to think of another example, actually. Perhaps a politician who needs to pass for one of the locals? Are you perhaps planning on becoming a Russian deputy?

Option two – 'the average learner'

OK, this one doesn't sound as interesting, I know, but that's exactly what we need! Let's start seeing pronunciation as a normal skill, and not some lofty master skill.

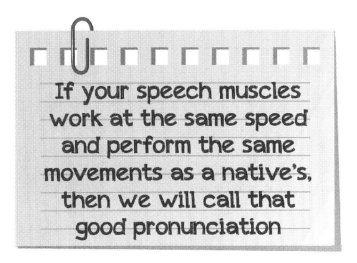

If your speech muscles work at the same speed and perform the same movements as a native's, then we will call that good pronunciation.

If your speech muscles work at the same speed and perform the same movements as a native's, then we will call that good pronunciation.

Will you have an accent? Of course! Having an accent doesn't mean that you have bad pronunciation. You shouldn't be a perfectionist. But, if your speech apparatus is working slowly and you are pronouncing completely wrong sounds, then your pronunciation isn't developed enough.

So what's the big deal if your pronunciation isn't developed?

What happens when you don't have the skill of pronunciation?

Without at least decent pronunciation, I really don't advise you go any further with the language – it will be really difficult! Pay attention here, I said 'decent' pronunciation, not a total lack of an accent. I am talking about the practical ability, the skill, to pronounce 'Russified' sounds at a normal speed.

The thing is, there is a link that you might have never considered: If your vocal apparatus can't pronounce Russian phrases quickly, then you will also find them hard to understand.

So, without the skill of pronunciation, not only will you have trouble speaking confidently and effectively, but you'll find understanding Russian hard too. The same thing with learning new words. Just how can you build your vocabulary if you can't pronounce the words properly?

Pronunciation sure is a tricky customer! And we won't make much progress without it. It doesn't matter how much vocabulary we develop or how much we study speaking or reading – we will still be driving on two wheels. And just imagine, all language skills are based on this secondary, 'decorative' (at the first glance) skill – on pronunciation.

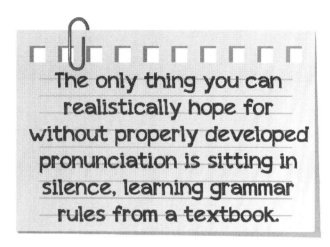

The only thing you can realistically hope for without properly developed pronunciation is sitting in silence, learning grammar rules from a textbook.

The only thing you can realistically hope for without properly developed pronunciation is sitting in silence, learning grammar rules from a textbook. That is more the study of linguistics rather than the way to master fluent Russian (you can read more about the struggles with Russian grammar in *Chapter 5. Grammar every day*).

Maybe you think I've been exaggerating the role of pronunciation?

Maybe you think that we can do just fine without it?

Nope, we just can't!

Our starting point: speech positions

Let's come back to this chapter's protagonist, Pierre.

By now you may have realised that Pierre started learning Russian in the 'wrong order'. And then he hit some serious trouble. He started by building his vocabulary and didn't do too badly – he knows a lot of words and can read well. But when it comes to listening, Pierre just doesn't make sense of speech.

Maybe you started like Pierre too.

Pierre (along with all learners) needs to start with Russian speech positions!

This is actually a very interesting concept, in my opinion. The problem is understanding what it actually means.

Did you know that it's often easy to spot foreigners in a crowd, even if they're not saying anything? One of the reasons for this is that their facial muscles adopt a certain position – a position that is optimal for speaking in whatever their native language is. For English speakers it might be one position and for Italians another and yet another for Russian speakers. We call this a speech position or 'stance' (like in sports).

Here's an obvious example for you: if a lady is getting to ready to dance the tango, she puts on her evening dress and high heels. If she is heading to the gym, she'll be wearing sweatpants and sneakers and so on. For different situations, we take on a different look. The same thing is true for speech patterns. One position when speaking Italian and another for Russian.

How can we develop our speech positions?
We can get a better understanding of the Russian speech position by remembering a favourite question of *almost all foreigners who come to Russia: "Why don't Russians smile?"* Can you copy a classic stoic, unsmiling Russian face? It's not very easy to smile from this type of 'position'; however, it *is* easy to speak Russian like this. Smiling is easy with a language like English – one movement and your face is already smiling!

Here's another little 'hack' that you might find useful. Try to do a stereotypical Russian accent. Yes, actually try speaking your own language with a heavy Russian accent. It's not as easy as it seems. You'll need to master the 'conversational position' and try to 'Russify' the sounds.

Please do *not copy* the Russian you hear in Hollywood movies! More often than not the actors are not speaking Russian with an accent, but parodying the language.

Language positions really are a tricky concept. It's almost impossible to explain and impossible to draw.

So how can we understand it and, more importantly, master it?

Time to experiment!

Experiment: how many Russian sounds do you know?

So what is all the fuss with these speech positions? Maybe we can just master some unfamiliar sounds and not bother going too in-depth? After all, Russian isn't birdsong.

Well, I propose we do a little scientific experiment!

To try this out, we'll take the word 'STOP' – a word we have in Russian and English. You would think the sounds were the same, right? Well, not quite.

Pronouncing 'stop' in Russian looks like this:

/S/ - tongue in lower position

/T/ - tongue in upper position

/P/ - tongue back in lower position

Now let's look at the word in English:

/S/ - tongue in upper position, 45 degrees

/T/ - tongue in same position

/P/ - tongue in same position

Can you see the sneaky bit here? To pronounce STOP with a Russian accent, when uttering T after S, you need to lift your tongue from bottom to top and then, to say the P, bring the tongue back down again. This takes time. When saying STOP in English, it's much quicker because your tongue stays in the upper position the whole time.

Try it yourself! If you can do it, you'll understand what a speech position is and you'll understand that 'identical' words between languages are not so identical after all.

It really is all about the positions, but to make it easier to think about, imagine there are *no identical sounds* in your native language and Russian. Different languages use different words, and it's the same with sounds. If you find one the same in your language, consider it the exception, not the rule.

'Unfriendly' Russian sounds

Now, don't rush ahead thinking you've mastered Russian pronunciation. The STOP experiment was just a very simple part of the big picture.

Now it's time for you meet the real bad boys of the Russian language. These are the sounds that you don't have in your native language. And there's no hiding from them!

You can, of course, try using the articulation charts, but I wouldn't advise you try looking at pictures of tongue placement and hoping to actually properly mimic these sounds. There aren't many people this works for. How many people who can't roll their R's have had a breakthrough after looking at a diagram?

Start simple: identify the sounds that are not present in your native language. These are your 'enemies'. You might find them hard to distinguish in speech. You find it hard to quickly and easily pronounce them.

So, what to do? First, you need to learn to perform the correct tongue movements in silence. Then you just need to practise, practise and practise some more. Practise is the only thing that will train your speech muscles.

Do you think learning proper Russian pronunciation from a book i: impossible? That's why I have a video lesson for you.

One student watched this lesson and said:

I was learning Russian for 3 months and now yc solved all my pronunciation probler in just 13 minutes.

You'll find the most useful 2 minutes of this lesson here:
www.LearningRussianMarathonBook.com >> BONUSES

The lesson is 100% free for readers of this book. It's your bonu

In the Bonus section –
www.learningrussianmarathonbook.com/#!bonuses/c1lzm
you'll find the most useful Russian pronunciation tips. Start practicing instead of just reading!

How we 'fixed' Pierre

Our friend Pierre came a long way in learning Russian, but the further he progressed, the more problems he encountered. Perhaps you can read Dostoyevsky in Russian, or maybe you're just learning Cyrillic. No matter what your level, if you have bypassed the skill of pronunciation, you will need to come back to the start – to the correct speech positions that will help you achieve fast, fluent Russian.

You don't have any issues with learning Russian and you are in the lucky 1% of people with some kind of genetic gift? Well, all the same, I would like to offer up a lesson that will come in handy, even for genetic polyglots.

Let's begin…

Speech position

To get the positioning correct, we'll need a non-standard, creative approach. I call it creative because, well, drawing speech positions is impossible and explaining them is even harder. We can only try to understand and 'feel' the process in action. And so, instead of waiting around for progress, we will do like Pierre did and take action.

We started with the 'unfriendly' elements – the hardest sounds. You need to hear about them once and remember them. This is quite easy as they stand out as it is.

The next step is a bit more difficult. We moved on to sounds that are in both French (Pierre's native language) and Russian. Stopping him from speaking Russian words with un-Russian sounds was no easy task. You probably know all about trying to read Russian words in Latin letters – far from fun or accurate!

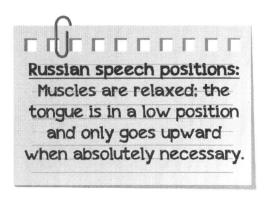

Russian speech positions:
Muscles are relaxed; the tongue is in a low position and only goes upward when absolutely necessary.

For Pierre (and perhaps yourself), here is a simple explanation of Russian speech positions: Muscles are relaxed; the tongue is in a low position and only goes upward when absolutely necessary.

Now, this sounds interesting, but looks a bit impractical, so the only thing to do with this knowledge about speech positions is to practise!

The focus: repetitions

In theory, we can break down the skills of speaking Russian and say, *"Here's a chapter on phonetics, here's one on grammar and here's one on reading."* Well, if you like to think about a language like this, then please, be my guest! The reality is that there is no skill breakdown. You either make use of virtually all language skills, you communicate – or you don't. In this exercise, Pierre was able to develop four language skills at once. 4-in-1. In my opinion, this is very effective *and* convenient. I can already hear you asking, *"What are these skills?"* Well, you'll know once you read this section. So, this is what our study method looked like:

Step one: we listened. We started with me reading a sentence as Pierre listened, without a text, trying to understand what he was hearing. If it was hard, he would just try to catch phrases, words or sounds. But not all at once. I read at normal speed, and then at a slower speed. For example: *"There is a boy."* We made sure he understood the sentence, correctly making out each word, then we read the sentence and, if needed, translated it. That is all there is to step one!

Step two: we repeated it – over and over. Enough with the listening, it was time for Pierre to start reading out loud. But again, not all at once – that would be too hard to do without making lots of mistakes. I would read a small excerpt, starting with one or two syllables, and Pierre would repeat. From syllables, Pierre would eventually build up to a full sentence.

It's very difficult to do, but you mustn't worry about mistakes! We all make mistakes. It's also tempting to repeat things quietly when you really need to repeat the words loudly and confidently.

As you can see, step two is also nothing too complex. Lots of courses and methods advocate the same approach. The only difference with me and Pierre was that we did multiple repetitions of the same phrases in order to successfully move to step three.

Step three: speaking at a natural speed. After working over a number of excerpts, it's time to move on to the next step. After all, what's the point in endless repetition? We're not training to be parrots!

Pierre read an entire section on his own. OK, reading is nothing special, true, but we weren't just reading like a school child. We were working on getting his speech apparatus working at normal speed – about 120 words per minute.

Do you need to be 100% correct and accurate at that speed? Typically, Pierre would make loads of mistakes and lose pace. That's OK, because he was learning to speak at 'real' speed, not some artificial textbook speed. He was speaking at native speaker speed. The most important thing was to maintain the tempo and intonation.

And that is about the lot. Each lesson, Pierre would read a page or two at a normal speed with acceptable pronunciation.

But for the reader, we still have some work to do. In fact, the most interesting part is just ahead…

You learned how to pronounce? Now forget about it

Is there anything else we can do? As it turns out, yes, there is. If you recall, earlier on I said that pronunciation is not some gift or ability, but a skill. And the most important part of this skill is speed.

It's very important to remember that you can speak and write Russian however quickly you like, but the speech positions must be correct. Only then will your sentences actually make sense.

So we will try to speed up.

Pierre tried speaking faster than a native speaker in the hope that normal speed would start to be extra-easy for him. For a very well-practised excerpt, we would speed up as much as possible to train his speech apparatus. If the norm was 120 words a minute, we would be trying to do **200 words per minute.**

Do you need to aim for that kind of speed without mistakes and stumbling? Of course we should aim for that, but even a native speaker would find this tricky. We aren't primarily looking for a perfect performance, but for something a little more interesting.

Firstly, from a purely **linguistic** perspective, the speech apparatus is taxed and trained. The brain learns to deal with a fast flow of inputs in Russian.

Secondly, it's about **psychology**. The student thinks *"Wow, look how fast I can go."*

Finally, this is a good way to get pumped up a bit. It's fun. You can't spend all your time on boring grammar drills without mixing things up a bit. People can't just do endless, monotonous work, not knowing what kind of results it will bring them in the future...

but when I look at some people doing the same things over and over again for decades, I start to have my doubts about people...

In any case, a good, engaging, well-organised Repetition lesson doesn't have to be boring!

How repetition helped Pierre and how it can help you

Repetition lessons are so good and so effective that I always recommend them. How could I *not* praise and recommend a lesson that combines 4 language skills in one! That's what I call intensity and effectiveness.

Have a look yourselves at what happens during a lesson:

1. We **listen** to Russian speech and train our listening comprehension.

2. We **read** – a lot and quickly.

3. We build our **vocabulary**. We don't just learn a list of new words, we learn words in context. We see and hear how they are pronounced and read.

4. And I almost forgot – we **pronounce**! You probably already guessed that a Repetition lesson is much more than a pronunciation drill – it is a total approach to training your language skills.

What's the main result? Of course you will improve your pronunciation and vocabulary, but more importantly, for the first time (perhaps ever), your speech muscles will be trying to work with Russian words at a normal speed.

Imagine how surprised your brain and speech apparatus will be!

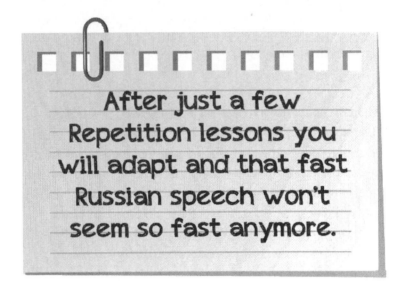

After just a few Repetition lessons you will adapt and that fast Russian speech won't seem so fast anymore.

Enough with the theory: here is your assignment

Repetition lessons are a great way of making a breakthrough in your learning. And they can help at whatever level you are currently at. Try it and don't put it off. You can give it a go today, right now!

Here's a reminder of the order:

1. Just listen one or two times and try to understand.

2. Read and translate if necessary.

3. From small 'chunks', starting with syllables, build the phrases. Repeat them multiple times, out loud.

4. Read with correct pronunciation at a natural speed (120 words per minute).

5. Speed up – forget about pronunciation and read a small section as fast as possible (200 words per minute).

What does this look like in practise?

Option one: work with a teacher. This is a solid option because a teacher can help you speed up and point out your weak points. You just need to explain to the teacher exactly how and what you want to do.

Another option: go solo. In this case, you'll need to be well disciplined to make sure you don't rush. Get some audio with text and work through it, phrase by phrase. You can then speed up and, if possible, measure your reading speed.

I think the best option is to use specially prepared audio lessons.

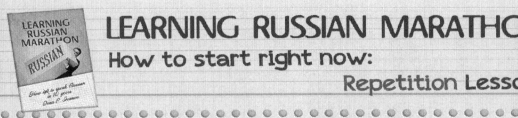

- Do you think my explanations are too long and theoretical?
- Do you need more help to start Repetition right now?
- Don't have any suitable audio?

OK, I have prepared this special video Repetition Lesson for you:
www.LearningRussianMarathonBook.com >> BONUSES

Now there are no more excuses holding you back
it's time to get started right away!

The lesson is 100% free for readers of this book. It s your bonu

Now you don't have any more reasons to put it off. Start right away! Here you can try: www.learningrussianmarathonbook.com/#!bonuses/c1lzm Repetition Lesson instead of just reading about it.

What result are we aiming for? Do you need to repeat each phrase 3 times or 100 times? A good result will be when you can read a full sentence or paragraph at 120 words per minute without missing a beat. If you find that too hard, try a less challenging text.

Does your pronunciation need to be perfect? Well, I think you probably already know the answer to that question. We probably can't get rid of any accent and every mistake right here and now. Just don't get stuck on one thing. Keep moving forward.

Our goal is fluency. When you can speak fluidly and achieve the correct speech position, your pronunciation will improve.

The secret to fluent and accurate pronunciation

Perhaps you got lost in the flow of thoughts and explanations. So here I'll run over the main 'secrets' that we covered one more time:

- Speech positions are like stances in sports. Different languages, like different sports, have different stances. The first step for you is to 'Russify' your speech position.

- Don't fall into the trap of thinking that sounds that look identical to those in your own language are spoken the same in Russian. As for the sounds that are not present in your native tongue, know them and remember them.

- Striving to be prefect, having zero accent, is a spy's job. The average student just needs to focus on smooth speech and pronunciation will improve, step by step, along the way.

- The skill of quick pronunciation is the base.

- On top of this base we build all the other skills.

- If you can't pronounce things quickly, you won't be able to understand Russian speech when you hear it.

- And now for the main 'secret': work on pronunciation in lessons, but when you hold a conversation, just forget about ideal pronunciation. Keep talking, formulate your thoughts, listen to your partner and feel positive about your communication!

In this chapter I have really been talking about how great Repetition lessons are. They truly are a powerful and intensive way of learning. You might get the impression that it's all you need to master Russian. Well, not quite! That's just the beginning. After all, you don't just plan on repeating phrases all the time, do you? You want to conduct conversations and answer questions fluently.

You'll find out about the shortest and fastest way to fluent conversation in *Chapter 2. Fluent autopilot Russian – dreams come true*

Chapter 2. Fluent autopilot Russian – dreams come true

Why are we so afraid of speaking Russian? Where does this stress come from? Get ready to try the most effective, stress-free way of speaking fluent Russian. Bonus Storytelling video!

Who: Mariko, Japan

The problem: A major language barrier. After a few years learning Russian, Mariko has good grammar but has come to associate speaking Russian with stress.

Notes: As is the case with a lot of Asian students, she is afraid of making mistakes. She prefers reading or writing.

The biggest disappointment

I've taken a delicate approach to everything in this book, but for this chapter, I'm going to be extra delicate. The reason for this is because of my personal experience...

My first presentation in English – I can remember it like it was yesterday. As bad luck would have it, everyone was there: the director, company representatives from Germany, France, the US and Korea. My very first presentation and I had all this pressure (when all I really wanted was to give my speech in an empty room)!

I wasn't nervous about the presentation itself – I had prepared and memorised everything – but there was one thing I was scared about: the Q&A after the presentation. And there were plenty of questions. So how did I answer? I took my time before answering while I calculated the answer in my head. What could the listeners have thought? That I had forgotten the answer? That I didn't know what I was talking about?

It seems so simple – you come up with a few phrases about a topic you are familiar with. But if you were never taught this, even a two-word answer can take time to think up.

At the time of my presentation, I had been learning English for 10 years. From the alphabet to words, grammar, lessons and more words. And in 10 years nobody ever taught me to answer basic questions simply and quickly!

What about you? Did you get taught to answer in fluent Russian?

You see, the majority of language learners practise all kinds of things, but not speaking naturally. For most people, the speaking aspect of a target language is the hardest part.

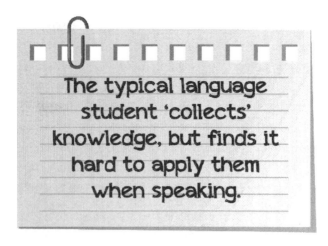

The typical language student 'collects' knowledge, but finds it hard to apply them when speaking.

The typical language student 'collects' knowledge. He/she knows a lot of words, rules and tables but finds it hard to apply them when speaking.

Just look at what happened to me when I was asked some simple questions. An intense memory and sentence-building process started in my head. Concentration, choosing the right words and then remembering the grammar rules. And the funny thing was, they could tell by looking at me that some serious 'brain work' was happening.

This is exactly what we *don't* want. We want to speak fluently, without tension – this is the goal for any learner.

It's worth stopping for a minute, thinking about this and then taking a step in the right direction.

Stop digging!

I want to start by saying that, if we spent countless hours learning a language with no result – that's our fault. We did this and nobody forced us into it.

This might sound cynical, but I have been there too and was in the same situation. I too used to complain about language barriers and how hard speaking was.

Now it's Russian language learners who complain to me about the same things. A guy who spent years learning Russian words and grammar (surprise surprise) and he still wasn't fluent. He asked me: *"Maybe I just need to work more on my grammar, can you recommend any good study books?"*

Well, I can't resist giving my favourite bit of advice to these types of questions (even if it does sound blunt):

First of all, if you find yourself in a ditch, stop digging!

Secondly, stop and look around for a minute. You've probably met people who are considered fairly adept at languages. They give off this impression because they take an approach that differs slightly from 'bad' language learners. Did you ever wonder what they do differently?

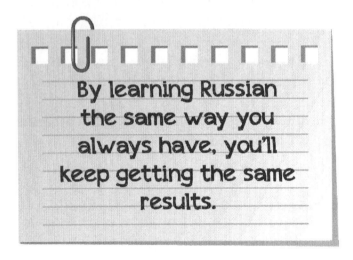

By learning Russian the same way you always have, you'll keep getting the same results.

Try doing things differently. If you're not happy with your results, you've got nothing to lose. By learning Russian the same way you always have, you'll keep getting the same results. We understand this; it's simple logic!

Two ways to terrorise a student

To avoid writing this chapter about myself (after all, this isn't a memoir or biography), I decided to select a 'victim'. Don't worry, right now our 'victim' is doing fine, perhaps better than yourself even, at least in terms of Russian language. But that wasn't always the case.

Meet Mariko from Japan. I'll say right away that students from Asia tend to be hardworking. They study hard and that is something I respect a great deal. However, for some reason, they aren't (generally) great Russian learners. The problem isn't with the language or the differences between Russian and Asian languages. Lots of students like Mariko are disciplined and, I think, quite conservative. They do as the teachers or study book says. And what usually happens is they end up following traditional, outdated methods.

So which route did Mariko take?

Like many other students, Mariko started with what I call the 'boring academic' approach (forgive me, linguists, for the generalisation).

Boring 'academic classes'

Let's take a little look at a standard language lesson: Students have their textbooks, study books and a vast amount of information. The teacher explains something, writes something down while everyone listens. *"Opens your textbooks to page 33, exercise 55..."* And what is exercise 55? It's a question-and-answer exercise – the student needs to answer a long question, remember all the rules and translate words.

If you're very lucky, the teacher might actually speak Russian from time to time (if he actually speaks it, which isn't always the case). *"My dad is an engineer"* repeats the class over and over. Is the classroom full of parrots? The thing with parrots is that they can pronounce things and repeat things, but they can't actually have a conversation. We want to avoid this – we want our brains to actually be engaged.

Repeating things out loud can be useful, but it won't teach you to think in Russian or to hold a conversation.

That's why students in this type of class end up leaving, sooner or later. It just depends on how persistent they are. Mariko left after two years without any visible results.

These students end up trying schools that use a 'progressive-conversational' approach (another new term in linguistics).

'Progressive-conversational' classes

In these classes Mariko was no longer silent, but it was still no good!

The main focus and approach of teachers using this method is to, literally, make the student talk. And just like in torture, they **have ways of making you talk!** Mariko was just another victim.

In these types of classes, there are no boring written exercises. The teacher might take his time, asking you to read some article or tell him/her something, but the goal isn't communication. The goal is to make you talk.

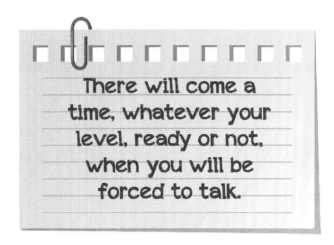
There will come a time, whatever your level, ready or not, when you will be forced to talk.

There will come a time, whatever your level, ready or not, when you will be forced to talk.

The more communicative students can manage this without any problems. The other students just want to get out of the class as fast as possible.

Using this method for too long is enough to make a student associate speaking Russian with stress and shame.

So did Mariko end up speaking relaxed, fluent Russian? Sadly, no. She held out a few months (which is quite good considering how hard she found it) and then just stopped learning Russian. Boring lessons coupled with stressful learning were too much to handle.

Stress – a sign of a bad teacher
Like a lot of learners, Mariko hit a dead end: speaking, especially out of class, is hard and stressful; learning in a quiet classroom is also no way to start speaking.

It's tempting to think that this is a complex problem and that modern scientists don't have an answer for us… but, wait for a moment! Billions of people on the planet all learned to speak their native languages without any stress at all.

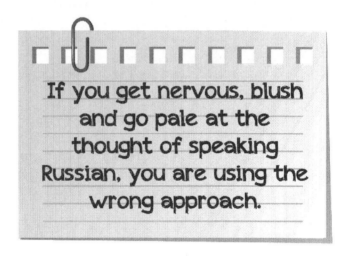

If you get nervous, blush and go pale at the thought of speaking Russian, you are using the wrong approach.

If you get nervous, blush and go pale at the thought of speaking Russian, you are using the wrong approach. I suppose you have a bad teacher.

To illustrate this point, let's imagine you are learning to swim. Have you met many 'progressive' swimming instructors who make their students shake with fear? Personally, I haven't.

When people learn to swim, they start with the most basic elements, at a low speed and a relaxed pace. Notice that these students don't learn to swim sitting behind a desk, and they don't get thrown into the sea to 'sink or swim' in their first lesson.

No, a swimming instructor uses special teaching techniques. I'd like to see this from language teachers too!

I can tell you this, though, when learning Russian, we can sacrifice complexity and correctness, but not speed.

Keep reading to find out why…

The real reason students can't speak fluent Russian

The educational system has played a mean joke on you. Most of the materials used in schools teach us to rush ahead.

I'd like to say: you're learning Russian *too quickly!*

After seeing and listening a text, most people think they have understood it all and need to move on the next, harder chapter. When they buy a textbook of sign up for a course, they think *"I'll finish this course and be level X"*, then they rush even faster!

Let's think for a minute: what's the difference between our native tongue and a foreign language? The main difference is effort spent – speaking and writing our own language is easy, automatic. Basically, there are no mental calculations involved.

Another example is basketball. If you get the ball in the net once, does that mean you can stop throwing the ball? That you need something more complicated? Of course not! Top players train and repeat the fundamental moves over and over.

It's the same with native speakers. After uttering some simple phrase, they don't magically start making things complicated.

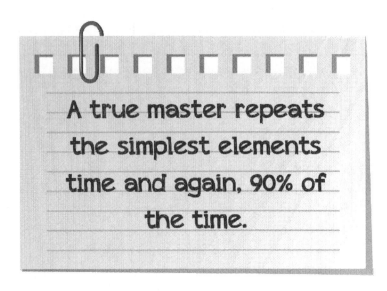

A true master repeats the simplest elements time and again, 90% of the time.

The typical language student (typical here meaning unsuccessful) does the opposite. They want to know lots of things, but it's all at a surface level. They try to become more erudite without being able to speak.

The slower you move when learning a language, the more solid your foundation for success will be. Now, this conclusion might sound strange, but it really shouldn't be: to achieve fluency, you must focus on depth – that's the way of the master.

The main indicator of a high level of linguistic skill is *not* the ability to quickly, mentally translate between Russian and your native language. No, your Russian will be fluent when you no longer need to translate things in your head. I'm sure that you don't think about it when you say 'Da' or 'Spasibo'. Well, that's the way it should be with the other 'slightly harder' phrases too.

Your textbook is fine. Here's what you really need to change

I'm sure you'll agree that something needs to change (otherwise you probably wouldn't have bought this book), but what exactly can we do?

Change your behaviour: you get advised to 'try this textbook', 'try this course', 'try this school'. You try changing language schools and 'trying harder'. You study twice as hard. The end result? Twice as much grammar and more stress when speaking. You lose motivation twice as fast.

Change your attitude. The end goal of fluent Russian is still far off, but you are demotivated and fighting the language barrier. This is where bloggers and polyglots advise you to 'think positive', to 'not fear speaking' and 'enjoy it when you speak Russian'.

Maybe everything is fine, but why can't you speak Russian?

Stephen Covey gave a very concise answer to this question in his book *The 7 Habits of Highly Effective People*. Changing your school or textbook won't do much and changing your attitude will make you feel better. But to elicit massive change, you need **shift your whole paradigm – change your whole language-learning system**.

Then you won't need to force yourself to study or worry about staying positive all the time.

It's time to dive in and change our paradigm, right now.

How we 'fixed' Mariko

Let's return to our friend Mariko, who wasted three years, hundreds of hours in classes and plenty of money. Stacks of dusty

Russian books sit in her closet while hundreds of unrelated words clutter her head. This is the sum total of Mariko's study.

Learning Russian after such a massive failure is no easy feat, but we did it by creating a paradigm shift.

Shift 1. Eliminate stress

We all know that stress holds us back. Sometimes stress *can* be useful – it can push us to breakthroughs, keep us on our toes. But for Mariko, stress was the main factor holding her back. Therefore, we had to get rid of conversation partners – and even teachers –without lapsing into silence. The only solution was audio lessons. This was the most painless way to break down the language barrier.

Shift 2. Even a parrot can repeat things

You will never magically learn to converse with a native speaker from just listening to podcasts and separate phrases. To speak, you must actively take part in conversations, not just repeat things out loud.

Mariko's audio lessons were based around questions, not repetition. The narrator has a lot of questions that need to be answered. The listener needs to think and respond.

Shift 3. Fluency is more important than complexity and correctness

We didn't ask Mariko the usual boring questions that you find in textbooks. We used very simple questions (maybe even one word questions) and the simplest possible answers. When answers are too long, they make the speaker think too much. This isn't what we want in real life, so we avoid it.

The narrator has a lot of very simple questions. You either know the answer or not, it doesn't matter. The main thing is giving simple and fast answers. How is that possible? You might think: *"I need hard, advanced sounding Russian."* So why are the questions basic? Because it's the simple questions that teach us to answer without pausing, without thinking. Speaking quickly, just like in a real conversation.

Shift 4. Deep learning with multiple repetitions

Mariko had gotten used to thinking that if she answered the questions in a textbook, then she had successfully completed the material and could move on. Perhaps you feel the same way.

This doesn't work for fluent speech. The skill of speaking needs to be automatic, with no hesitation. So, with Mariko, with each exercise I would ask a lot of questions. It was an almost endless flow of questions. Mariko repeated one audio lesson a few times per day for a whole week.

This amount of repetition makes the student learn the material on a deep level, which is what brings us closer to fluency. Remember, fluency is our goal, not memorised answers to questions.

We'll call this type of lesson Storytelling lessons. What exactly does a typical lesson look like?

- The narrator asks a lot of very simple questions.

- The student answers out loud (and preferably loudly).

- There are no right or wrong answers. The goal is to answer quickly and simply.

- Knowing the answer does not mean you are ready to move on to the next unit. We are building a skill and need to repeat things over and over until we achieve automatic fluency.

Why this worked for Mariko and how it can work for you too

Mariko was totally uninterested in storytelling to begin with.

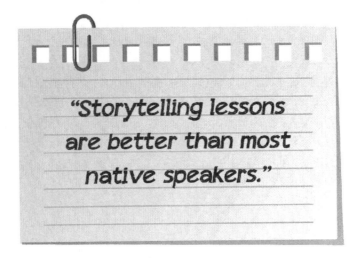

"Storytelling lessons are better than most native speakers."

I bet her it would work and she agreed to try it. After just two weeks of using storytelling audio lessons she was convinced and told me: *"Storytelling lessons are better than most native speakers."* I love to repeat her words!

Storytelling really is more effective than most lessons with native speakers because:

- You can access your lessons any time, at any place

- They don't interrupt you

- They 'listen' carefully and produce the correct response

- They never make fun of you or criticise you

Jokes aside, this really is one of simplest and most effective approaches. With proper study of these materials, your language barrier will soon be a thing of the past.

Storytelling lessons can be practised with a teacher (on an individual or group basis), but, in my opinion, recorded audio lessons are a highly effective – and cost effective – way of learning too.

Are you ready to take the first practical step?

Now it's time to for you to decide whether or not you are ready to shift your Russian learning paradigm. Or are you happy with where you are right now?

For those who are ready for change, here's a small example of a Storytelling lesson so you can see how it works, step by step.

The teacher makes a statement, something like *"the boy wants to go to the theatre"*. You just listen, not memorising anything – you don't need to strain to try and recall any details. You can just smile and nod like in any normal conversation. In an ideal scenario, the teacher will come up with something really crazy or funny, for example *"the huge cat wants to go to the theatre"*. The thing about this is that, the more wild the statement, the easier it is to remember. This makes the process that extra bit more efficient.

Then, the teacher asks: *"Who wants to go to the theatre?"* You don't need to recall some large and complex sentence to answer the question. Just say the first thing that comes to mind, for example 'girl', 'cat', 'I'. The key is to answer quickly and, of course, out loud!

The teacher then bombards the student with questions like 'who?', 'to where?', 'a boy or a cat?' He does this to get a quick answer, not necessarily a correct answer!

Here you can try Storytelling Lesson:
www.learningrussianmarathonbook.com/#!bonuses/c1lzm
instead of just reading about it.

How long do we do Storytelling and what result are we aiming for?

You can perfect the art of conversation forever; there's no 'end' to it. These lessons can be repeated time and again for a long while. You don't need to aim for super-complicated questions and answers. Spend the bulk of your time practising and repeating the basic, simple parts.

Your road to mastery will look something like this:

- Learn to understand questions and answer them.

- Learn to answer simply.

- Gradually increase your speed, try to get ahead of the teacher. Try and compete with the native speaker narrator.

- Make your answers more complicated, but remember: this is the very last step.

Secrets to speaking fluent Russian

To make things crystal clear:

- Simply parroting things after a teacher will not teach you to converse. We don't need blind repetition.

- Answers to textbook questions and forced conversational practise will not break down your language barrier; quite the opposite, they will reinforce it.

- Lots of simple questions and answers will help you learn to speak quickly and fluently.

- As strange as it sounds, up to a certain level, Storytelling will be more effective than simply speaking to a teacher – even if he/she is a native speaker.

The thing most common concern I hear about Storytelling sounds like this: *"I doubt that this Storytelling will actually teach me the language of Tolstoy and Dostoevsky."*

Well… you are right to have your doubts. Storytelling is your training ground – a safe place where you will build confidence, speed and, eventually, smash your language barrier. As for adding in complexity, beautiful speech and exploring the depth of the Russian language – that's what we'll be looking at in *Chapter 6: Why you hate writing Russian.*

Chapter 3. Don't understand Russian? Just smile and nod!

Is Russian speech really that fast? Why is it so hard for us to understand? Find the source of listening comprehension problems and try out a simple solution.

Who: Peter, Australia. He knows plenty of Russian words, his grammar is solid and so is his reading.

The problem: When people speak to him in Russian, he just smiles and nods because he doesn't understand the spoken language.

Note: He thinks that Russian is a really beautiful language, but it's just too fast.

Troublesome listening

Anyone who has studied Russian knows how hard it is to understand a native speaker. It's not because you don't know enough words. You might know a million words but still find it impossible to understand a native speaker…

Take my friend Peter. He stubbornly refuses to speak Russian. He's an interesting case – he knows how to speak (his pronunciation is actually really good), he knows plenty of words and he knows Russian grammar better than most Russians. And yet he still goes out of his way to avoid speaking Russian. But why? He just doesn't understand spoken Russian. For Peter, not understanding and having people repeat themselves is embarrassing, shameful even. But is this an isolated incident? No way – I see this kind of thing all the time!

You see, it's not so hard to understand your Russian teacher or audio materials in class. So why do native Russian speakers have to talk so quickly and make it so difficult to understand what they're saying?

Take movies, for example. When you watch a movie with subtitles, it's easy to understand. But as soon as you turn off the subtitles, the words become difficult to separate and understand. Everyone is just talking too fast!

But what is it that makes 'real' Russian speech so hard to understand?

Good news: speed testing Russians

When we don't understand something, we ask for it to be repeated more slowly. We like to think that it's all about speed. Of course, when we get hit with a 'waterfall' of incomprehensible sounds and words, we say to ourselves: *"There's nothing wrong with me, it's just that native speakers speak way too quickly."*

So what about the audio materials used in most courses? They'll be fine for us. But where will we ever hear speech that slow in real life? After all, our end goal is not study materials, but real, living, breathing Russian.

As strange as it sounds, Russians are slow speakers. To prove my point, I propose a little experiment.

We will measure the speed of spoken Russian in comparison to English (although if you speak another language, you can conduct a similar test using machine translation; it's quite simple).

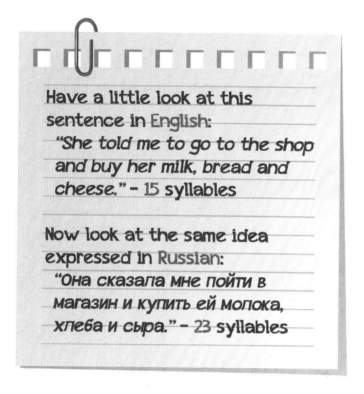

Have a little look at this
sentence in English:
"She told me to go to the shop
and buy her milk, bread and
cheese." - 15 syllables

Now look at the same idea
expressed in Russian:
"Она сказала мне пойти в
магазин и купить ей молока,
хлеба и сыра." - 23 syllables

We can clearly see the Russian sentence is longer! In English, there are 15 syllables. In Russian, there are 23.

Well, this looks like good news for us! **Russian words are longer and, in theory, you have more time to understand what is being said.** It means that speed isn't the main factor that makes it difficult to understand Russian speech.

The bad news for you and our friend Peter is that we can't just 'blame' our audio troubles on the speed of Russian speech. We need to dig deeper and find the root of the problem.

Funny history: How linguists compared military language

Following the end of World War II, American linguists analysed the military language used by Americans and Japanese. It turned out that Japanese soldiers spent more time on commands in critical situations than their American counterparts – Japanese words and phrases were longer. The Americans hypothesised that this could influence the outcome of battles in which fractions of a second count. After looking at Japanese, they moved on to Russian, and, as you might have guessed, time spent on commands in Russian was longer than in English too. So did this spell disaster for the Red Army? As it turns out, no, it didn't. After some more studying, the linguists found that, in critical situations, Russians switched to… Swearing! This was, in fact, a great move, as Russian curses can replace whole phrases with just one word or a few words!

What Peter, and probably you, were advised to do

It's fairly obvious that the problem is with understanding spoken speech – the same speech that students are advised to listen to more often. A teacher suggested that Peter watch movies in Russian. So he watched a lot of movies and TV shows. It helped, but his progress was still very slow…

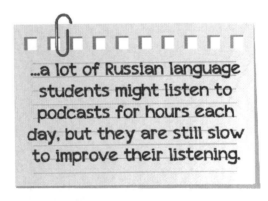

…a lot of Russian language students might listen to podcasts for hours each day, but they are still slow to improve their listening.

Just like my friend Peter, a lot of Russian language students might watch movies and listen to podcasts for hours each day, but they are still slow to improve their listening.

When a teacher advises a student with listening problems to simply listen more, I find it quite strange and not particularly intuitive.

Let's use another comparison, swimming, for example.

Imagine if you couldn't swim and you arrived at the pool to hear: *"OK, you can't swim. I think you just need to swim more – here's the pool. Just make sure you swim every day at home."* Then you get charged for your swimming 'lesson'!

In my mind, this is what language teachers are doing when they tell struggling students to simply listen more.

What we need is to understand why our listening comprehension takes such a long time to improve, even when we practise listening all the time. When we watch movies, we don't usually understand much of what's being said. If we get frustrated, we cheat and use subtitles. Eventually we might just lose interest altogether.

Now, please don't get me wrong here; I'm not saying that you shouldn't watch movies in Russian! Even if you don't understand everything, it's a lot of fun and helps motivate you. BUT you have to understand that it is a very passive, slow way to learn a language.

Returning to our comparison of listening and swimming, remember, if you are enjoying what you're doing, keep it up! But, if you start to 'drown', then it's time to make some changes.

Remember, if you keep doing the same things, you'll keep getting the same (often less than optimal) results.

Time for some unhelpful tips

If you've been paying attention, you'll notice that I've told you things that should be fairly obvious. None the less, I know that people miss things and repeating key points never hurts.

So, I'll say it once again: you need skills. I'm sure that most of you have plenty of grammar knowledge and know plenty of words, and yet, in live speech these words go over your head.

We've talked about the traditional methods of simply 'listening more because listening is important'. But all the same, you have probably noticed that after watching your favourite shows in translation multiple times, you still can't catch the sense of most of it. At this point, you might do one of two things: realise that you are just not understanding or turn on the subtitles. But how can we call it listening if we are using subtitles?

It's better to listen and break down a 5-minute audio clip 25 times than to watch an entire season of your favourite TV show 1 time.

If you love watching movies and shows in Russian, remember that it's better to listen and break down a 5-minute audio clip 25 times than to watch an entire season of your favourite TV show 1 time.

If you're lucky, your favourite show will have the same characters using the same type of language in each episode. This is great for us because people are built to learn things by being exposed to them over and over again.

Another thing worth remembering for lovers of podcasts and listening to things in the background is that all your attention needs to be focused! If you want to reap rewards from your efforts, you need to be 100% focused on what you are listening to. You have to make sure that you can hear every sound.

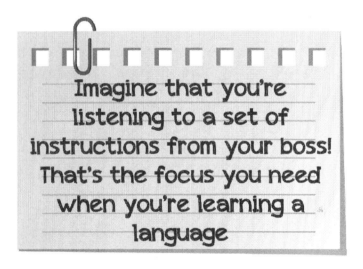

Imagine that you're listening to a set of instructions from your boss. That's the focus you need when you're learning a language! You can't skip over any words or sounds that you don't understand. You can't miss a detail.

Now you're probably thinking that I'll just tell you to pay more attention and not get distracted; after all, the title of this section is 'unhelpful tips'. But that cliché advice is just too unhelpful.

To listen successfully, we need to look at the brain: our brains evolved to avoid any extra activity and energy expenditure whenever possible. When you listen, you can't give your brain a chance to relax and get distracted!

Don't worry, after just one more page, I'll tell you the right way to listen…

Looking at the unobvious: the interdependence between speaking and listening

For most people, language skills are divided into different categories. You might think: *"Ah, my pronunciation is good, but wow, my listening needs work."* This way of thinking is convenient for teachers as it makes it easy for them to sort their students into different groups.

We believe that listening and speaking are two totally separate subjects, like math and physical education.

You may have also noticed that I refer to listening as a passive activity, which would suggest there is an active counterpart, correct?

There is an interesting theory behind this. It is believed that when we listen to another person, our speech muscles make micro-movements – movements that we can't see and don't notice ourselves. To understand what's being said, we need to repeat it on a micro-movement level.

With this in mind, we can see that the problem for a lot of people who say they 'can't understand' is not that they have hearing problems. Their problem is that they can't keep up on a micro-speech level. And why can't they keep up? Because their speech movements are incorrect or just too slow. But what's even more likely is that their micro-movements are both incorrect AND too slow!

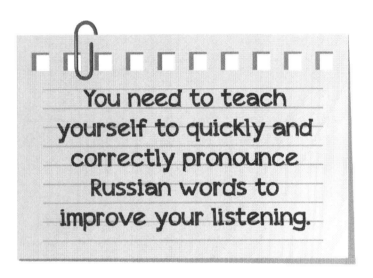

You need to teach yourself to quickly and correctly pronounce Russian words to improve your listening.

The only conclusion we can draw is that you need to teach yourself to quickly and correctly pronounce Russian words to improve your listening.

Luckily for you, you won't need to test and measure your speech patterns and vocal output or conduct other experiments. You can just take this theory and put it into practise so you're no longer a 'passive' listener.

Now it's time to start 'actively' listening.

How we 'fixed' Peter

I imagine you're pretty confused right about now after reading those last chapters! So much advice and so many conclusions – it's a lot to keep track of…

It might seem impossible to put it all into practise. That's why we're going to keep things simple.

Take kids, for example. A child listens to an adult and then gradually starts to repeat things – first single sounds and words. When a child starts out, his efforts don't sound anything like adult speech, but he still gets excited and keeps up his linguistic 'adventures'. Can you see what I'm hinting at here?

Let's come back to our old friend Peter. He's a great example because there are literally thousands of 'Peters' out there. Me and Peter took three steps:

Step one: I don't understand, but I'll try to repeat
You may remember that Peter wasn't a total newbie in Russian. He knew a little bit about Russian phonetics and knew some words.

I had a small text that I read to Peter. To make things easier for him, I read it slowly. My task for him was simple: all he needed to do was repeat what he heard. It didn't matter if he understood the text or not and it didn't matter if he missed some parts.

I told him he was going to go back to basics and needed to repeat what he heard as I was saying it. I got Peter to put on some headphones so that the sound of his own voice didn't distract him. He focused only on listening. His pronunciation wasn't important and neither was missing words or sounds.

The important thing here was repeating what he heard out loud and loudly. To start off with, you will probably miss most of the words and sounds. That's OK. If you can't repeat what you hear loudly, you can whisper it. The main thing is **to not remain silent**.

What did Peter achieve with this method? He improved the micro-movements we discussed above and he also learned to single out words in a flowing sentence.

Step two: synchronised reading out loud

At some point, we all want to understand the gist of what we're hearing (for most of us, this happens sooner rather than later as adults don't like repeating incoherent sounds all day long). As mentioned before, we also need to learn to single out words from the general 'flow'.

Coming back to Peter, I moved on to using texts, sometimes with translations. I would read and he would follow along verbally, simultaneously repeating everything out loud.

It was OK if Peter missed some of the meaning or grammar aspects – that wasn't the point of the exercise. The most important thing was that the general meaning of the phrases and words was understood.

I read the text slowly on purpose to make the first reading easier. But generally, it's better when a teacher starts with 'natural' speed right away.

What was I aiming for with these exercises? The main goal was to teach Peter to 'move with the flow' of spoken Russian and understand. Yes, we were looking at the text, so it wasn't 100% listening. But the text didn't bog us down. We kept moving. This now brings us to step three.

Step three: I understand, and I'll repeat

In step three, we were still listening and repeating, but without texts. We would repeat things simultaneously and loudly. We also added in other factors: now we had to repeat with maximum fidelity to intonation and tempo.

Peter had to pay attention to the listening aspect, manipulating every sound. This is not the same as listening to 'background' audio.

Doing the audio exercise the first time, learners will probably find it difficult. They might only manage a few sounds or words. But don't worry, after a few days of regular practise, students will get faster and more accurate.

Let's review the steps in order:

1. We listen to Russian speech (without a text) and repeat the sounds, syllables and words simultaneously. We repeat the audio a few times. You don't have to understand everything.

2. We take the text and break it down, translating if necessary. We learn to 'swim' in the 'flow' of Russian language.

3. We take away the text, listen and repeat simultaneously. Repeating things 100% simultaneously isn't always possible, of course; there's always some delay. At this point, you'll need to be strict with yourself to get the best results.

We'll call the combination of these three steps 'Vocal Listening'.

How Vocal Listening helped Peter and can help you

I'm sure that you can see the hidden meaning behind these exercises. In order to understand a native speaker, your vocal apparatus must be able to work very quickly with Russian sounds. Not just your ears. Your vocal apparatus has never been as fast a native speaker's vocal apparatus. Even slow speech was too fast for it.

For many people, the problem is not that they can't hear well. If you can hear native speech, you can also hear foreign speech. The speeds are almost the same. The problem is that your vocal muscles don't know how to work with Russian sound, in *"Russian mode"*.

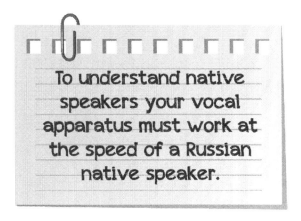

To understand native speakers your vocal apparatus must work at the speed of a Russian native speaker.

To understand native speakers your vocal apparatus must work at the speed of a Russian native speaker.

The main goal of the exercise was to encourage the student to feel comfortable listening to Russian.

The student has to listen very carefully, trying to catch every sound. It's a lot different than listening to something in the background.

Doing this kind of thing for the first time can be really challenging, and the typical student might only be able to manage individual syllables or words.

Don't worry, though. With time and regular practise, learners are able to repeat what they hear in real time.

Enough with the theory, here is your assignment

Here's a lesson that you get for free! This exercise is great because you don't need a teacher to help you with it. You might need someone to evaluate your progress from time to time, but it's not a must. All that you need is motivation, audio and a text.

Select an audio track that has one or more native speakers talking about something. Make sure it's not too easy or too difficult for you to understand. You should understand about half of what is being said. The speed should be close to native Russian speed. After all, you don't want to learn to speak slowly, do you?

Go through each step of the Vocal Listening exercise a few times. Be ready, though, it will be hard to begin with.

So now there are no more excuses holding you back – it's time to get started right away!

How long should you practise Vocal Listening? What kind of result do we want?

You don't have to be perfect. It doesn't matter how bad you sound. When you start, you will probably only be able to repeat individual syllables, but it is important that you try to copy the Russian speaker's intonation, speed and accent.

Here's the ideal scenario: you are practising Vocal Listening with headphones, listening and repeating things out loud. Anyone who overhears you should be sure you are speaking Russian fluently and confidently. They might even mistake you for a native speaker!

Once you reach that level, normal Russian speech will sound calm and relaxed to you. You'll understand almost everything without much trouble and actually have time to think about what you're hearing!

Secrets to understanding spoken Russian

I really do want us to understand each other. But here's the thing: I think it's important that adults understand not just WHAT they should do, but WHY they should do it. With this in mind, I'm going to sum up all the main points from this chapter:

- Native speakers speak very quickly, but that's not the main reason you can't understand them.

- Russian words are longer than English words and the Russian language is slower than English.

- Lots of passive listening is not very helpful at all.

- The reason it's hard for you to understand something in Russian isn't that you have hearing problems!

- To properly understand Russian speech, you need to train your vocal apparatus to work faster – like a native speaker

Here's a great reader question I received: *"So will we completely understand Russian after completing the Vocal Listening exercises?"*

Here's my answer – you'll start to understand Russian sounds, words and phrases. But understanding the meaning of every speech or text is a completely different story...

Chapter 4. Memory like a super computer?

Is your memory good enough to hold a huge vocabulary? Find out what you need to do with your word lists to guarantee you'll understand what you hear and be able to use your new vocabulary.

Who: Emma is always learning new Russian words. She wants to have a huge vocabulary so she can speak advanced Russian.
The problem: Emma complains that she has a bad memory and it takes a long time to recall the right word in conversation. She just wishes Russian words could be a bit shorter.
Notes: Emma actually has a great memory. We need to figure out what her real problem is.

Thousands of Russian words

In June 1990, Samuel Garibyan set an impressive new record. He memorised and recalled 1000 randomly chosen words from English, German, Urdu, Dari, Farsi, Pashtu, Bengali, Esperanto, Arabic and Spanish. You can look it up in the Guinness Book of Records.

Clearly Samuel has a pretty impressive ability. Imagine how quickly you could speak fluent Russian (and other languages) if you could do that too. After all, to speak Russian you need to know thousands of strange, long words. You know it, I know it and Emma sure knows it.

So yes, the story of Samuel's record is really impressive, but I think we need to remember another story, one far more common for people like me, Emma and perhaps you too.

This story is about a schoolboy who thought that if he learned all of the letters of the English alphabet, he would be able to speak English. Of course, he was mistaken – just knowing a foreign alphabet doesn't mean you'll be able to speak the language (you and I know this all too well!).

His teacher at school told him that he also needed to memorise words before he could learn to speak English. So he memorised a couple of thousand words. You won't believe it, but it turned out his teacher was wrong. Even with all of his new words, he didn't know how to hold a conversation in English. All he had was a bunch of almost useless information in his head. He couldn't use this knowledge to converse freely in English.

A bit later in this chapter you'll learn the scientific reason for our schoolboy's linguistic failure, but right now I need to make a confession: that little boy was me.

So yes, you might be surprised, but having a good memory isn't enough to learn a language.

You have a great memory, but it's not going to save you!

I'm not going to make any sweeping statements here. Suppose we decide to rely on memory when learning Russian. We'll take a closer look at how good your memorising abilities would need to be: Imagine you decided to learn 1000 Russian words so that you can hold basic conversations. You're a pretty smart guy or girl and you've got tons of motivation. This won't be too hard, right?

Good, let's move on to the fun part!

The first thing you will need to know is that Russian nouns change their form depending on the case. There are 6 cases, so there are 6 different forms for each noun in the singular, as well as 6 in the plural. Just to use a simple word like mama [mother] you need to memorise a table of 12 words.

Verbs are even worse. Let's try the word 'go'. The dictionary gives us two options: idti or hodit'. And don't forget about the 6 basic verb forms: I go - idu, you go - idesh', they go - idut, etc. Then there's the past, present, and future tense. Even a simple verb like 'go' has dozens of different combinations to memorise.

So actually, to memorise 1000 Russian words, you really need to memorise a whole lot more.

On the one hand, this might come as bad news to you (if you really didn't know this).

On the other hand, now you know your memory is probably just fine.

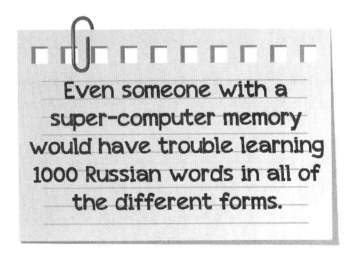

Even someone with a super-computer memory would have trouble learning 1000 Russian words in all of the different forms.

Even someone with a super-computer memory would have trouble learning 1000 Russian words in all of the different forms.

But just hold on a minute! If that's true, how did hundreds of millions of people (I'm referring to native Russian speakers) manage to memorise so many tables?

Well, allow me to state the obvious for us all: native speakers don't memorise tables and word lists.

So why don't we do like the natives and try and recreate some of those native results?

How we did it in the Middle Ages

I have my own theory behind why we so often believe that learning a foreign language consists of three steps:

- Step one: learn the Russian alphabet

- Step two: memorise lots of Russian words

- Step three: learn some grammar, especially the cases

People started learning languages by the old-school method of 'alphabet-words-grammar' many centuries ago. Let me paint the picture for you: a classroom, pupils tightly packed in together behind desks and a strict teacher pacing the classroom. Talking and fidgeting is strictly forbidden. Pupils repeat things out loud and the atmosphere is oppressive…

And what are these pupils doing? Learning Latin. People who went to school in the Middle Ages had to learn Latin because it was considered to be the foundation of all sciences.

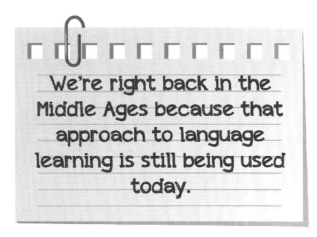

We're right back in the Middle Ages because that approach to language learning is still being used today.

We're right back in the Middle Ages because that approach to language learning is still being used today.

Lots of modern learners are still using these dated learning techniques – I've been there, Emma's been there and maybe you have too.

According to this dated learning style, you first learn the grammar rules, then you memorise many words, and you don't get any practise in the target language.

And with Latin, you didn't even need conversation since all you'd be doing was reading manuscripts.

Right now, you might be thinking: *"Have we really not managed to think up any better way of learning?"* Well, don't worry, we have, and there are far more effective alternatives. You can learn a living language with the goal of being able to hold conversations, interact with the culture and meet real people! In this world and this modern approach, there's no place for memorising words.

If you do choose to memorise a list of translated words, just remember that you're using a method for learning Latin, a dead language.

A helping hand from linguistic theorists

Let's come back from the stale Middle Ages to our modern world. This world has armies of scientists who dream up endless numbers of theories and concepts for everything under the sun.

The theory we're interested in is on procedural and declarative memory. Unlike a lot of the other theories floating about, this one can be really helpful for language learning.

Suppose we only want to use declarative memory and go the route of declarative learning. This basically means we memorise facts. A list of words and grammar rules from a text book would be a good example of this.

And what about a pure procedural approach? In this case, we'll only learn by doing things in practise, placing emphasis on skill, not bothering with factual knowledge.

Which approach seems 'correct and contemporary' to you?

Allow me to answer that question with a metaphor: Two men decide to learn to drive. The first one spends days learning the rules of the road (declarative learning). The second one just decides to get behind the wheel and learn (a fan of procedural learning).

Neither one will get far because to drive successfully, you need a mix of road rules and skills.

You and I can easily see this!

We understand this, but for some reason, we don't apply this when learning a foreign language...

Obvious facts and pointless experiments

I noticed that obvious facts retold in a clear and simple manner surprise people the most. So now I shall try and surprise you in the same way (although I know it's not easy)!

So, you never studied your native language by using lists of words. Your parents never gave you a list of words and said, *"Learn these 20 words and you'll start speaking."* More importantly, you never learned new words with the help of a translation – what translation?!? It's your native language!

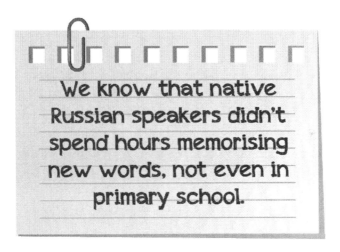

We know that native Russian speakers didn't spend hours memorising new words, not even in primary school.

So here's an obvious fact for you. We can learn a new language fluently without even using translations. We know that native Russian speakers didn't spend hours memorising new words, not even in primary school. They never bothered learning thousands of case tables and conjugations.

They had a far more natural approach, and it was this approach that made them fluent native speakers.

The opposite approach – the one where we memorise lists of words – should be called the unnatural approach. Perhaps this is why our brains start to resist and switch off when we start trying to memorise unfamiliar words this way.

If you don't believe me, we can test this theory using a simple experiment:

First, count to 10 in English. Then do it in Russian or any other language that you know. Pretty easy, right? Now count to 10 by alternating between English and Russian: «one, dva, three, chetyri, five…» Was that more difficult? It took me about 5 times as long. More importantly, it took a lot of energy and it wasn't much fun for my brain. You do the same thing to your brain every time you try to learn Russian words with a translation.

This brings us to an important conclusion: translation is what stops you from doing effective study. Mixing two languages into one piece of information seriously slows down your brain down.

Here comes another useless question: **How would you feel if all your memorising efforts couldn't be put into practise?**

It would be terrible! We would feel terrible and deceived. That's what happened to me and Emma too.

But why does this happen?

Well, we already know the scientific explanation! A bunch of facts without context (like knowing all the rules of the road) don't give us the necessary skill (driving a car). In a nutshell, the Russian language learner is using declarative learning alone.

To make matters worse, **the average language learner doesn't even use declarative memory effectively!**

Imagine for a minute that you want to learn the whole Russian dictionary. Pick a simple phrase like *"How do I get to the metro?"* and try translating it word for word into Russian. I can almost 100% guarantee that your translated phrase would sound unnatural to a native speaker, and it might not even make sense at all. Words learned separately can rarely be combined together like this.

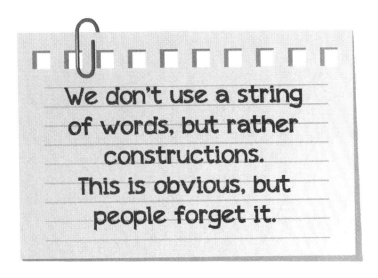

We don't use a string of words, but rather constructions.

This is obvious, but people forget it.

How we 'fixed' Emma

At the very start of this chapter, I promised to tell you what Emma's problem really was. Emma, the student who couldn't memorise enough words. Perhaps you've already got an idea of what the true issue is.

Her problem is not memorising words, it's *using* the words. She collections knowledge, but isn't honing her language skill. She knows all the rules of the road, but actually driving is something completely different.

Probably the only thing you could do if you *did* manage to memorise the whole Russian dictionary would be to read.

So, let's make some changes to your system of trying to build up a huge vocabulary.

Step one. Give your brain a rest: context instead of translation

First we had to stop mixing two languages. How did we do this? We took the standard list of translated vocab and took away the translation. Now, I'm not saying you should learn Russian words without understanding what they mean; quite the opposite, in fact. What you need to do is put the words and phrases into context, which is where they belong. This way, you'll have a much better understanding of their meaning. The context should be either written text or audio.

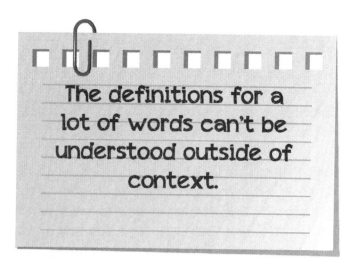

The definitions for a lot of words can't be understood outside of context.

The definitions for a lot of words can't be understood outside of context. Open up a dictionary and you'll find several options for each word. Sometimes there are dozens of answers. There's no point studying a word out of context!

We used a relevant Russian text instead of a list of words with translations. That's the first transformation. The text should match your level in terms of difficulty. The text will be a good fit if you find a few unknown phrases on each page. Some unknown words and phrases you will be able to guess and others will have to remain a mystery – their time is yet to come! But the words that you can guess should be your main focus. Grab them and mark them. These are the lexical gems that will help increase your vocabulary.

I want us to understand each other 100%. There is nothing inherently wrong with translating phrases and words. Our goal is not to memorise new words and phrases without knowing what they mean.

But there is something I want to avoid at all costs: Firstly, I want to avoid mixing languages together (like writing words and translations together on one page) – this is hard work for our brains. Secondly, I want to avoid taking single words out of context (because we lose the exact meaning).

Translation doesn't replace context. Trying to directly translate foreign words isn't just ineffective, it's pointless too. Perhaps you've heard that Eskimos have tens of words for snow in its various forms and states. Imagine trying to learn these words without their Eskimo context – how would that work out?

A similar example of this with Russian is trying to learn the names of Russian dishes. Even if you memorise the names of all the dishes, a translation won't be of much use! If you've never tried kholodets or bortsh, you won't really know what to expect until you try them. If you directly translate 'dressed herring', or literally herring under a fur coat, you won't have any idea what it is!

Step two. Becoming grammatically correct
OK, great, we've stopped painfully pulling words from text and audio. We'll leave some of the unknown ones in their place for now. Life is a bit easier – less learning the dictionary and more contextual learning.

At this point, Emma and I (and hopefully you too) took the next step to dramatically improve our productivity.

Here's an example of what we did: when we came across a phrase, like Kak proyti v biblioteku? (How do I get to the library?). Our memory breaks this simple phrase down into a list of four words: kak, proyti, biblioteka, v (how, to get, library, to).

The alternative is clear: **you can avoid breaking it down and just memorise the whole phrase, thinking about it as a whole.**

Are you worried that it's going to be more difficult to learn a long phrase, rather than a single word? Is this approach really more effective? Well, let's take a closer look: If you ever need to ask someone how to get to a library in Russia:

- you'll save a lot of time and effort because you won't need to remember how to conjugate the verb proyti.

- also, you won't think about which preposition to use (v, k or do).

- and best of all, you won't need to worry about memorising the case ending!

Another nice plus is that you won't end up with some strange sounding Russian phrase, for example something like 'which path may me take me forth to the library'.

You'll sound like a normal person, and not some mythical wizard from a fairy tale.

You'll sound like a normal person, and not some mythical wizard from a fairy tale.

For lovers of scientific theories, when we start memorising phrases as a whole in this step, we're effectively using our declarative memory.

Here's a computer analogy: Using this approach, you don't have to fill your brain with the words (separate cells on your brain's hard drive), plus complicated case and conjugation tables. You also don't need to stress your brain with tough calculations (which case to use, which preposition etc.).

By filling just one 'memory cell' in your brain, your information is ready to be used right away. Now you just need to learn how to access this *"memory cell"* quickly!

Step three: Don't invent pronunciation

Just because this is step three, it doesn't mean it comes right at the end – quite the contrary! To be honest, we really should think about this whole process completely differently. What we are doing is adding text support to our study of new phrases in an audio context.

Emma would quite often forget about this step, as you might too, along with a lot of language learners. What most people do is listen to how a word is pronounced a few times and leave it at that.

But what if you are a visual learner and it's easier for you to remember information with your eyes?

There's a simple answer:

When you read a word, your vocal muscles produce micro-vibrations. (You can learn more about this in *Chapter 3. Don't understand Russian? Just smile and nod!*).

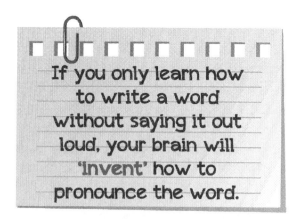
If you only learn how to write a word without saying it out loud, your brain will 'invent' how to pronounce the word.

If you only learn how to write a word without saying it out loud, your brain will 'invent' how to pronounce the word.

Unless you listen to the correct pronunciation first, your own pronunciation probably won't be very good. Most likely, you'll have an accent and will say the word slowly.

It's especially important that you hear a word at the same time that you see how it is spelled for the first time.

And what's even more important is that you don't forget to repeat the phrase to yourself, preferably as much as possible, out loud and loudly. After all, you're learning to speak Russian, not listen to Russian!

But it doesn't end here: practise makes perfect

There's a good Russian saying that goes, basically: 'repetition is the mother of skill'. It's quite obvious that, regardless of the system you use, repetition is necessary. People don't usually remember things the first time. Well, maybe vivid experiences, but definitely not Russian words.

We need repetition to successfully retain information like words or phrases. We also need repetition to develop a skill, like fast and accurate pronunciation.

So how can these wise old proverbs about repetition help us?

Sadly, they can't! The wise old phrases don't quite go far enough and actually tell us how much repetition we need.

But what about science? Well, there are some theories and experiments, but the conclusions differ. There is only one general scientific consensus: when seeing something new for the first time, the most effective way to remember the information will be to repeat it, first every couple of seconds, then increasing the intervals to an hour, a day and then a week.

For example, you see the new phrase. The ideal intervals to memorise it would be 10 seconds, 5 minutes, 30 minutes, 2-3 hours, 1 day, 2 days, 1 week, then, say, 3 weeks.

But how can we time the intervals correctly in practise?

Do we need a special system, program or table?

Well, I don't want to sound pessimistic, but I've yet to meet anyone who has managed to successfully use these repetition intervals in their learning.

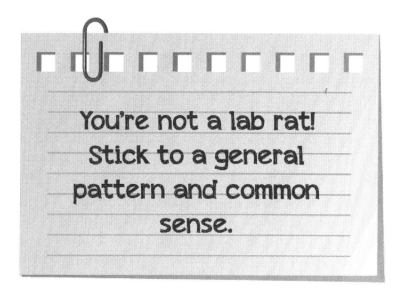

You're not a lab rat!
Stick to a general
pattern and common
sense.

When looking at the different theories for optimal memorising, you need to remember one important thing: you're not a lab rat!

Stick to a general pattern and common sense. You don't need to precision time your repetition intervals to get great results. Your brain is capable of great things without any super technology!

Why this helped Emma and why it will help you too

I think you might have started reading this chapter expecting some super technology hack that would help you memorise the whole Russian dictionary without lifting a finger (maybe learning while you sleep – the dream of students everywhere). Am I right?

Well, in any case, I'm going to run down the main points from this chapter one more time, but I'll keep it short!

So, at the start, **we stopped mixing two languages**. After all, Russian words with translations next to them can 'mix up' our brains.

Having gotten rid of the translation, we needed some way of understanding what we were looking at. The answer: putting the words in a text that we can understand that helps us **use context** to figure things out.

We stopped trying to learn words separately and started **focusing on language chunks**. These are the ready-made building blocks of language. They are grammatically correct, sound natural and are ready to use.

Then we took texts and focused on listening and pronunciation, moving **from knowledge to skills**.

Finally, we tried (I have to stress this) to follow an effective **routine of repeating** new words and phrases. Following a pattern of minutes, hours, days and weeks yields a good result with minimal time and effort. So it all looks simple, no? It sure is simple – this is why it will work for you time and time again.

But please, don't leave anything out of this system! Everything needs to be used together, otherwise it just won't work. If the system stops working and you get upset, feel free to write me an angry message. I'll be upset too! Instead of that, let's use this system correctly, starting right now…

Enough with the theory, let's get practical

Step one. Right now, go and get a Russian text that fits your level. You'll need some accompanying audio (maybe a podcast or audiobook).

How do you know what fits your level? In an ideal world (which is hard to achieve in reality), the text should have a few new words for you on every page.

Step two. Read the text, preferably listening to the audio simultaneously.

You should guess the meaning of the words from the context. If you guessed the word without translation, that's great! Consider it a little win. This will be the most sure-fire way to understand a word and its place in the language. You don't need to write out a translation. Don't write it on a list, in a book or any other place; just mark it in the text.

So what about the words that you still don't understand? Don't look them up in the dictionary! Your reading time shouldn't be spent digging around in a dictionary. We used to do something like that in school. Our teacher would say: *"You need to learn to work with a dictionary.*" Well, I couldn't work with one, and so what? And we aren't working with a dictionary either, we're reading and listening.

If you didn't come across any new or incomprehensible words, then your text was too easy and you won't learn anything new.

If you didn't really understand much of what was going on, you need to find a text that is a bit easier.

Step three. You mark the words and phrases in the text so that you can repeat it, without going through the whole text. You run over the highlighted phrases and try to recall the new words. Sometimes you might have to reread the whole sentence or paragraph in order to remember the meaning.

It's hard to not pick up the dictionary because we're so used to continuously checking meanings. We're afraid of missing a new word.

Trust me, if this word is really useful and important, you'll come across it again soon and understand its meaning.

Secrets of an amazing memory

If you read this chapter, it will be no secret that:

- It's impossible to learn Russian by memorising words. There are too many different forms. Our memories can't handle even a basic number of words.

- To get the best results, we need to use a mix of declarative and procedural memory (facts and skills).

- When you memorise language structures instead of words, you're making better use of your declarative memory (and you'll sound natural when speaking).

- You shouldn't separate writing and pronouncing new words. If you read a word without first hearing it and how it should sound, your brain will create its own poor pronunciation.

I think the real secret to an amazing memory is that you don't really need it to successfully learn a language. Of course, a great memory helps. But the reality is that we all managed to master our native languages without a phenomenal memory. Use your brain properly and you can master Russian too.

Chapter 5. Grammar every day

What's the hardest thing about learning Russian grammar, and what can we do about it? How can we use a textbook properly? Here you'll discover the path to mastering the habit of grammar. Grammar Variations video bonus!

Who: Greg, USA
The problem: Greg's Russian consists of pauses, mistakes and more pauses. His written test results are great.
Note: He's an expert on Russian textbooks. He has a whole collection of them and can tell you in-depth about the pros and cons of each.

Mastering Russian grammar in 7 days

A title that like sounds like the perfect advert! Everyone wants to master the grammar quickly. In fact, if that was the name of this book, it would probably become a bestseller.

However, I have to be honest with you and admit that I don't know how to master Russian grammar in 7 days. This book isn't about tips and hacks that magically get you speaking Russian. I don't know any hacks like that and I'm sure nobody else does either.

Russian grammar is complex, illogical, hard to memorise and easy to forget.

I'm also not going to be sugar coating reality for you: Russian grammar is complex, illogical, hard to memorise and easy to forget. It is most likely very different to your native language's grammar – which makes life even harder.

That doesn't mean that the process of learning Russian grammar is equally as daunting. No, in this chapter we'll talk about a better way to learn Russian grammar.

Imagine how strange it would be if there only existed one route to mastering Russian grammar. With so many teachers, linguists, textbooks and language courses, it would be crazy.

Of course there are lots of approaches to grammar. Are you happy with your results? If not, it's time to change things dramatically. Once you do, you'll see a lot of your grammar troubles start to disappear before your eyes.

In this chapter, I'm going to show you how you can make learning grammar a lot more manageable, but first...

Some scary grammar facts

We're going to get started with the hard parts – the hardest of the hard. After all, knowing a problem is half the battle.

Having said that, I hope I don't put off any new students or depress any long-time learners as we dive into these 3 *especially* unpleasant parts of Russian grammar.

Part one: cases

Needless to say, cases are extra difficult for students who don't have them in their native language.

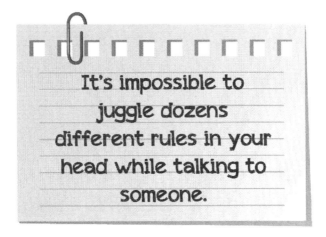

It's impossible to juggle dozens different rules in your head while talking to someone.

Even if you are good at memorising lots of rules, this doesn't always make speaking easier. It's impossible to juggle dozens different rules in your head while talking to someone.

Here's an example: the word mama [mother].

If she's not there, we say net mamy – the genitive case.

If you're calling for mamu – the accusative case.

If you miss mom, you are thinking o mame – the prepositional case.

Oh, and I forgot to mention that instead of learning 6 forms for each word, you really need to know 12. Don't forget that sneaky plural!

It's really amazing that a 4-year-old child can speak a language with so many rules, without even thinking about it!

Part two: verb aspects

For example, you use govorit' when you are speaking right now or when you speak on a regular basis. But you use skazat' when you are talking about something that you said or will say once. In other words, each action requires two different verb forms.

So how are these verb forms created?

VERB ASPECTS
Sometimes, you just have to add a prefix:
    Читать -> Прочитать
    Писать -> Написать
    Делать -> Сделать
Other times, the suffix changes:
    Решать -> Решить
Sometimes a completely different verb is used:
    Говорить -> Сказать

Part three: Verbs of motion

Here's an example: hodit' [to walk]. It seems like a simple verb, but look at how many different prefixes can be used with this one verb!

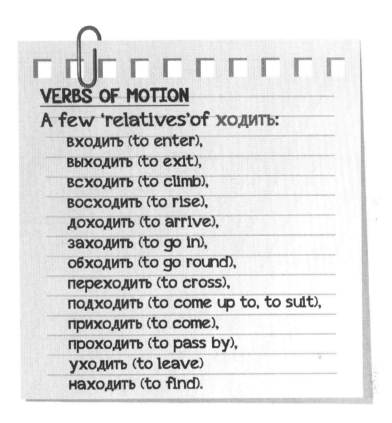

VERBS OF MOTION

A few 'relatives' of ходить:

входить (to enter),
выходить (to exit),
всходить (to climb),
восходить (to rise),
доходить (to arrive),
заходить (to go in),
обходить (to go round),
переходить (to cross),
подходить (to come up to, to suit),
приходить (to come),
проходить (to pass by),
уходить (to leave)
находить (to find).

Many of these forms also have several meanings, which makes it even more complicated. English phrasal verbs, such as 'break down' and 'get up', are kind of similar to Russian's prefixed verbs.

During conversations, you'll need to quickly recall what each of these forms means, or risk not understanding what your friend is saying.

The problem with Russian grammar

I have a little test for you. You see, I like to have fun with Russian language students and ask them: did you learn Russian grammar? Can you prove it to me?

As proof, I usually hear all about the six cases, verb conjugations and other bits of grammar knowledge that most native speakers don't even know (it's only the linguists, Russian teachers and school pupils that know about this stuff).

From hearing these types of answers, I understand right away that the person in question sees grammar as a kind of 'collection' of knowledge.

In other words, they think that mastering Russian grammar means memorising endless lists of rules, exceptions and tables.

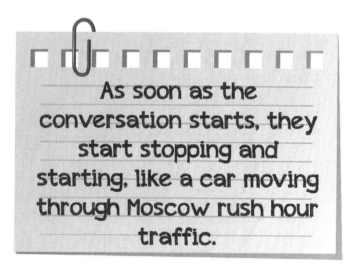

As soon as the conversation starts, they start stopping and starting, like a car moving through Moscow rush hour traffic.

I can spot this type of student a mile away – by the way they speak. As soon as the conversation starts, they start stopping and starting, like a car moving through Moscow rush hour traffic. You see, they're taking time to think in between answers, their brains are working like a computer running calculations. And even with all the pauses, they still make mistakes!

After struggling through a normal conversation, they conclude that they need more grammar and more tables!

Now, after all my criticisms against knowing the rules and linguistic terminology, you might be wondering: what do I expect as proof of good Russian? For me personally, it's the fluent usage of grammar constructions, not a fancy list of grammar terminology.

Grammar is a skill, not just passive knowledge.

You won't be able to overcome any of the linguistic hardships we discussed by simply 'collecting' more knowledge. Imagine how impossible it is to juggle all those tables and rules during a real-life conversation.

So I'll say it again: Grammar is a skill, it is not passive knowledge.

Students make life even harder for themselves by continuing to use outdated or ineffective approaches. There are plenty of publishing houses that publish language books year after year, and it's always the same old stuff. Very rarely do we get to see a language book that does something differently – that breaks the mould.

Because of this, language students end up using the same old methods and getting the same old results.

How to choose the right grammar textbook

Allow me to start with an analogy: riding a bike. It might seem that riding a bike is much easier than learning the Russian language, but in actual fact, bike riding is also just a skill. It's just that you learn this skill in a different way.

So, imagine if this was how you learned to ride a bike: you have a teacher and you learn some independent movements. For example, you move your right leg downwards then you practise this a few times on a stationary bike. You then move to the next movement and so on. You have a book that describes all the moves a cyclist performs.

How fast do you think you'll learn to ride a bike using a strategy like that?

Yet, as obviously ineffective as that seems, all the standard Russian grammar books teach us this way. And it's not just textbooks, it's audio courses, programs, language-learning apps and more.

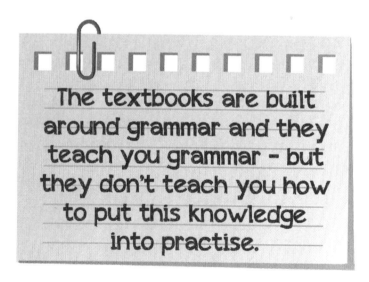

The textbooks are built around grammar and they teach you grammar – but they don't teach you how to put this knowledge into practise.

The textbooks are built around grammar and they teach you grammar – but they don't teach you how to put this knowledge into practise.

Your cycle teacher gives you homework – get on the stationary bike and pedal three times. You go home and diligently do what you are told. How much pedal homework like that would it take to actually have you riding a bike?

Sadly, that's what most language books do. They can't break away from the cliché and popular methods of language teaching. After 15 minutes of explaining a new grammar concept, the average Russian teacher gives you some practise exercises for homework.

I had a chat with a teacher and it went something like this:

- *"Why did you give us this assignment?"*

- *"So the student practises the new rule and reinforces the topic. It's obvious."*

- *"So after doing these exercises, a student can start using these concepts right away in conversation?"*

- *"Of course not, 10 exercises is nowhere near enough."*

- *"So when will the student start to actually put this into practise?"*

- *"…"*

As you can see, this teacher knew perfectly well that the exercise wouldn't yield any result. And the authors of many textbooks on the market know the same thing.

Have you ever come across a textbook that didn't just give you knowledge and tell you the rules, exceptions and so on? Have you ever seen a textbook that actually taught you to use this information in conversation? Please let me know if you have, because I sure haven't.

Now, things might sound pretty hopeless, but it's not all so bad. A grammar textbook is simply a tool. And like any instrument, it has its applications – we just need to use it *correctly*.

A bit later in this chapter, I'll teach you how to make the most of any grammar textbook.

Two ways to learn grammar: the effective and the endless

I just spent a few pages convincing you that you can't learn to ride a bike from books, just like you can't master the skill of grammar. It's a dead end, a waste of time, energy and motivation.

We can do things differently – we can go the route of the native speaker. A native speaker is simply someone who has, for many years, been exposed to Russian. This way is much better than the usual rule-learning route. You'll actually see results, although it is still a long process think how many years it takes to acquire a language.

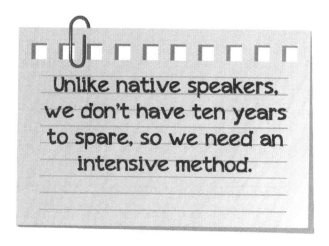

Unlike native speakers, we don't have ten years to spare, so we need an intensive method.

Unlike native speakers, we don't have ten years to spare, so we need an intensive method.

It's not just about saving time (some students are happy to spend forever on a language). The more intensive your learning, the quicker you see results and the better your motivation is. You'll stride more confidently toward your goal, not giving up halfway.

I'd love to create some intrigue and tell you there is in fact a secret recipe, but there isn't. What we do have is a widely-known and tested approach.

The ingredients to *this* recipe are:

First: Exposure. You need to be exposed to proper grammar (written and spoken) as much as possible. 'Absorb' the language, just like a native.

Second: Language constructions. I mean groups of words and phrases that you can use in conversation. There is no point in learning forms (cases and conjugations etc.) without context. It's unnatural and difficult.

Third: The so-called variations. When using language, one and the same thought needs to be converted into different forms. For example, first and third person (I am going…he is going…), tenses (I was going…I will go), in the imperative (go!) and so on. This is what makes grammar hard. You need to learn to change things up when learning grammar.

The variation of the examples and the other points I just mentioned are what make up a highly effective and intense grammar solution.

It's this kind of approach that helped my friend Greg, and it can help you too.

But who is Greg, and what was he struggling with? Well, allow me to introduce you...

The fight with grammar

After one of my presentations, a man came up to me and, in very slow Russian, said that he liked my grammar philosophy, but thought that it would be impossible to put my ideas into practise.

"How can I speak Russian if I don't know all the rules?" – he asked.

I said: *"Greg, say something to me in your native tongue, anything you want."*

He answered something along the lines of *"I'll go for a walk if it doesn't rain."*

So then I asked him: *"Now list out all the grammar rules that you just used."*

His response? *"Oh, I don't know."*

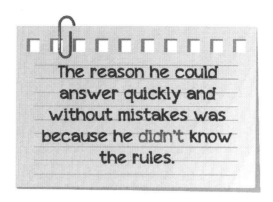

The reason he could answer quickly and without mistakes was because he didn't know the rules.

The reason he could answer quickly and without mistakes was because *he didn't know the rules*. He used a ready-made construction in his head that he knew how to use.

The real truth is that not knowing, or, more precisely, 'forgetting' grammar rules, is the only real path to fluent Russian.

Greg's head was full of math, not language. First he learned the theory, then he tried not to forget the formula to his linguistic 'problems' and yet he still made mistakes.

No surprise, really; we don't solve math problems in our heads in fractions of a second (well, apart from certain geniuses). That's not what our brains (or Greg's) were meant for.

How we 'fixed' Greg

Here's what we did: We changed up everything, dramatically. We said goodbye to the 'mathematics' that were holding him back. Finally, we put down the grammar and textbook – the last thing we wanted was another textbook.

Step one: Time out on the textbook and rules

This part is fairly self-evident. Greg had spent years learning all sorts of grammar, but hadn't reached his goal of fluent Russian. What's even worse, after spending all that time on grammar, he still made lots of mistakes. Greg's brain just couldn't handle the sheer volume of knowledge in his head and so he would make very simple mistakes. So in light of all this, we put the textbooks on hold (Greg may hit the books again in a couple of months after 'rehabilitation').

Step two. From theory to practise

In an ideal world, a student would be exposed to 'live' language before even learning any grammar structures. But more often than not, a Russian student comes 'armed' with an arsenal of grammar knowledge, just like Greg!

What students like Greg need is practical representation of what the Russian language really is. We don't need endless names of grammar terms from a textbook, we need real-life constructs.

So how did we make the change?

Original story. We took a short text, a dozen of short sentences at most. For example: *"She left her home…"*, feminine past tense.

Greg just had to listen carefully and concentrate.

We could read the story or we could listen to it. We could even find the meanings to all the unknown words, this is all fine. This is the long route that I talked about earlier.

With this in mind, we didn't just switch to another text or story. We made Greg's lessons super intense and included plenty of variety, for example:

First person. I told the story as if I was the main character. I used the masculine gender: *"One year ago, I left my home…"*

Every day. What if we were talking about my daily routine? *"Every day I leave my home…"*

Future tense. Now we talked about events in the future. Imagine this is what I'm going to do next weekend: *"Tomorrow I'll leave my home…"*

Order / imperative. Now we went over the imperative form, for example, when talking to a colleague: *"Billy, could you please leave your home..."*

You can use a lot of different variants. Now you have to admit, this is far closer to real life speaking that exercises in some dusty grammar book!

As I mentioned before, these exercises are intense. That's why we use small text sections and look at them from different perspectives. We're not reading *War and Peace* - we're laser-focused on small texts.

Step three: deep skill reinforcement

We agreed to view grammar as a skill to acquire. This is a skill that takes more than two repetitions to hone. Not even ten repetitions are enough.

Greg listened to the same variations over and over again. He wasn't memorising or analysing – just listening intently. After all, he didn't want to start fighting to recall things the next time he spoke Russian. He just wanted to feel that 'this is the way correct Russian sounds. And that was exactly what happened!

This is a method of grammar acquisition that I highly recommend – we'll call it Grammar Variations. The exercises can look different but the goal is the same – looking at a piece of language from different points.

What's so good about Grammar Variations?

So why is this method so effective? Why do I recommend it?

The first thing is, it doesn't clog up your memory with grammar algorithms. It doesn't scare you off or make you doubt yourself.

This is one of the main differences between it and other grammar learning techniques.

Focused variations show how Russian is used in different scenarios. This is a practical approach to the language and stands in contrast to the theoretical side (learning tables and forms of words).

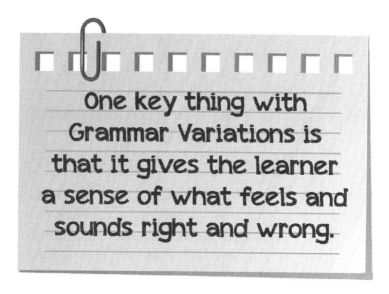

One key thing with Grammar Variations is that it gives the learner a sense of what feels and sounds right and wrong.

One key thing with Grammar Variations is that it gives the learner a sense of what feels and sounds right and wrong. Just like with our native language, we can tell what 'sounds right' without knowing all the grammar rules in depth. This is the same thing we are striving for when listening and speaking Russian.

A textbook will never give you that 'feel', but Grammar Variations will – not right away, but with patience and time.

What to do with the textbooks – burn or bin?

"Bin them". "Give them away". "Burn them". These are just some of the more extreme suggestions that I've heard, but we won't be so hasty just yet.

So what *should* we do with the grammar textbooks? You might think I'm telling you that grammar is completely evil: *"Denis thinks that if we could just get rid of grammar, then everything would be okay..."*

Well, that's not what I'm saying at all.

The problem is that grammar textbooks can be very 'dangerous'. If you don't know what you're doing, they can create more problems than they solve.

Here's what I suggest you do.

First, you need to understand what a particular piece of grammar does. You need to understand why it's there and how it's used. For example, think about the past tense for verbs. You know why we need a past tense in a language. You know when it is used and why it is used. You can easily give some examples.

If you understand all of that, you can read about it in a textbook.

A good exercise to try is speed reading a grammar textbook. Pay attention to the grammar themes that you understand. You might think 'I've seen this before' or 'Ah, that's why they say it like that'. You don't need to memorise anything or dive in really deep – doing that will only put you off and demotivate you.

When 'speeding' through the grammar like this, just skip the parts you don't understand. If a certain piece of grammar doesn't mean anything to you, then it's too early to read about it in a textbook. For example, perhaps you see a chapter called *"Reflexive Verbs"*. If you can't give at least a few examples, or don't know where or why reflexive verbs are used, then all the textbook theory will not help you. It's just going to confuse you even more, slow you down and make things more complicated.

And what about the exercises? Well, you can do the exercises at the textbook, just don't attach too much importance to them. Think of them as a mini-quiz that will help highlight your grammar strengths and weaknesses.

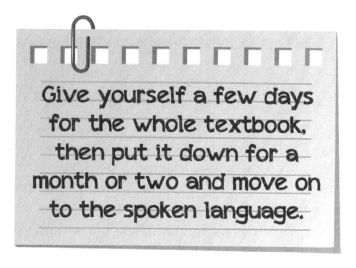

Give yourself a few days
for the whole textbook,
then put it down for a
month or two and move on
to the spoken language.

Give yourself a few days for the whole textbook, then put it down for a month or two and move on to the spoken language. In this time, you'll recognise new grammar forms and even pick up how to use them. Then you can come back to the textbook and cement your theory. Here's an easy rule to remember: language comes first, then grammar.

Enough with the theory: here is your assignment

I bet you have a grammar book, maybe even a few. So here's my proposal - we ban the grammar books starting today. Put the textbook aside for, let's say, 3 months. Try taking some drastic action and see how it works for you. Slap a sticker on your text-book that says *"Do not open until this date"*.

Try out the approach that I described.

I'm absolutely convinced that after 3 months you will not regret your decision. I want you to see just how much easier it is to use a natural approach when learning grammar rules and exceptions!

Take a minute to gather yourself, focus your efforts and throw yourself into Grammar Variations.

How to do it? You can use this example when working with a teacher, although finding a teacher who knows and understands this approach is another story...

Audio lessons are just as effective, possibly even more so as you can listen to them over and over again, at whatever time suits you.

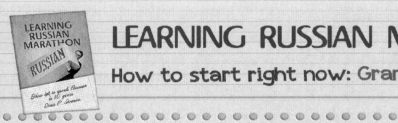

Here you can try Grammar Variations Lesson:
www.learningrussianmarathonbook.com/#!bonuses/c1lzm
instead of just reading about it.

How to maximise your results?

I recommend listening to these lessons periodically. It's not worth memorising these texts as that won't really be of use. Listening to them one or two times is fine, but the best way is to study a small section and go in-depth.

Remember, we agreed that grammar is a skill and we don't master skills with a few repetitions.

The more you listen, the more Russian grammar will sink in. it will be easier for you then, when you do open your grammar book, to recognise the proper terms for things that you have already been exposed to and, possibly, know how to use.

Grammar learning secrets

Russian grammar is only complex and scary when you see it in a textbook. As soon as you move to a practical application, things become easier. Here are a few reminders to keep you on track:

- The golden rule: The more grammar rules you know and try to use, the slower you will speak.

- A *"mathematical"* approach to a language does not work. You can't solve language 'equations' in your head during a conversation.

- To be fluent *and* correct, you must learn to see grammar as a skill, not a collection of knowledge.

- Learning how to change forms within context for a single word does more harm than good. Only learn language constructions as a whole.

- Strive for intense, in-depth grammar practise. Don't rely on native speakers – it took years for them to assimilate their grammar.

The Grammar Variations approach (as opposed to 'knowledge collecting') will give you the feel for correct and incorrect Russian grammar usage.

So what do we do with this? Start talking right away?

Have a read of *Chapter 2. Fluent autopilot Russian* – dreams come true to see how and when I recommend starting to speak without losing motivation and hitting a language barrier.

Grammar practise in conversation is great, but what if you don't feel ready yet? Well, in this case, you can find your best 'first steps' in *Chapter 6. Why you hate writing Russian.*

Chapter 6. Why you hate writing Russian

Is there any point to written exercises, or are they all boring? Find out just how written exercises can help you sound like a native speaker.

Who: Xavier from France. A big fan of Russian language and literature. Especially fond of Tolstoy and Dostoevsky.

The problem: Xavier's Russian sounds a lot like Google Translate – grammatically correct, but somehow unnatural and a bit 'off'.

Notes: For Xavier, there is no punishment worse than written exercises. They demotivate him and put him to sleep!

Dostoevsky would not approve

Go open Facebook and find the Dostoevsky page. It has a couple of million likes. Leo Tolstoy is no slouch either and is just as popular. Generation after generation has enjoyed masterpieces like *War and Peace, Crime and Punishment, And Quiet Flows the Don* and more. For many foreigners, these legendary works are the first point contact with Russian culture.

The effect is that Russian writers of the past are still inspiring millions of people all over the world to learn Russian. In return, modern-day Russian teachers are weighing them down with written exercises.

And that love for Russian turns into hate!

Ask any grownup language learner who goes to a language school or courses – they'll usually tell you that teachers who set lots of written exercises are 'bad' and the lessons are 'boring and useless'.

So many times I've heard the following:

"We sat down and got sheets with written exercises."

"We had a whole day of writing today and it was so draining."

"We don't learn to speak because we spend all our time in our notebooks."

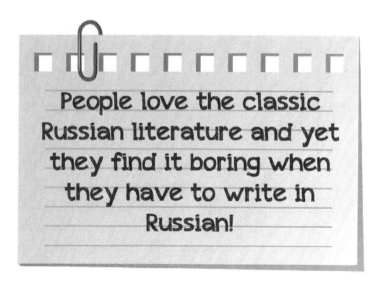

People love the classic Russian literature and yet they find it boring when they have to write in Russian!

How could that have happened? People love the classic Russian literature and yet they find it boring when they have to write in Russian! I can imagine what Tolstoy would have to say about that! Stroking his beard, I can almost hear him: *"Those who cannot properly express themselves in writing cannot be considered literate at all!"*

In most universities and language courses, written Russian gets turned into a useless and pointless affair. In reality, this should be an enjoyable skill that you polish over time – one that makes your language 'beautiful'.

Writing helps organise your knowledge and new skills in your head. When we write, it is like we are analysing and remember the language constructs we know. You don't need to be fast when writing, so you can just focus on writing correctly! If your pronunciation is polished, your vocab good, grammar OK, but you can't speak as smoothly and nicely as in your own language – this is where written Russian will help you.

Can a written essay really help you with spoken Russian?

Yes it can! So let's not disappoint Tolstoy and Dostoevsky. Let's dive into this chapter and learn to love writing in Russian.

Written exercises: easy for the teacher, useless for the student

What comes to mind when I say: *"OK, now we will do some written exercises"?* What do Xavier and other students think when they hear this?

Looking into a Russian class, we often see everyone sitting in silence, working in their textbooks. A lot of Russian classes look more like a maths test: brains are busy analysing exercises, working through grammar rules – the same way you solve math problems. One of the worst exercises is the type where you have to 'fill in the gaps'. I'm sure you are all familiar with this because you see it in most classes.

So, do we actually master any skills with these types of drills? Sure, the skill of inserting missing words! What about mastering language skills? No way!

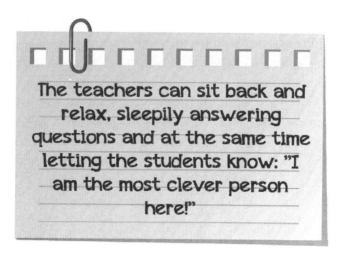

The teachers can sit back and relax, sleepily answering questions and at the same time letting the students know: "I am the most clever person here!"

The teachers can sit back and relax, sleepily answering questions and at the same time letting the students know: *"I am the most clever person here!"* These types of lessons are a dream come true for them! You won't have to worry about these types of lessons anymore. In fact, I'm sure that, when you finish this chapter, you will have a whole new outlook on written exercises.

How Xavier and Tolstoy write essays

For a minute, let's forget that we are learning Russian and that our language isn't as rich as a native's. We are going to look at a special example classroom. We are going to sit Xavier down next to Lev Tolstoy in a typical language class and give them a typical grammar exercise – essay writing.

This is what this type of exercise would look like:

First: Tolstoy doesn't like the topic

Our students, Tolstoy and Xavier, are set a topic, for example 'complain about service you received in a restaurant'. Xavier tries his best, even though he doesn't find the topic very interesting and, really, he doesn't have much to say about restaurants as he doesn't even eat out, but what can he do! The teacher said it had to be done and that's that.

What about Tolstoy? He would most likely be stroking his beard and planning some 5-volume epic novel. But no such luck!

Second: volume overkill

In our essay, the students have to express their thoughts in no less than 200 words and no more than 300. Imagine how sad that makes Tolstoy, who's used to writing 100,000-word epics. Xavier is OK, though – for him, 200 words isn't a lot and he can write that in no time.

Third: correcting Tolstoy's mistakes

The essay has been written. Next, an editor will be checking it and then handing it back to the students. There were lots of mistakes and they were all corrected. I don't know what Tolstoy thought when he got his essay back with corrections on almost every line, but when Xavier got his work back, his conclusion was: *"My X, Y, Z grammar topics need work and, by the looks of it, my Russian grammar is really bad."*

Last: publication and reading

Actually that's it – there is no final step. All the essay work remains in some textbook or in a folder and that's where it stays. The result of all that hard writing is something that nobody even needs. Well, real writers would never accept something like that! They would re-read their works, think about what they'd written…

What kind of results do we get from essays like this? After all the work of writing, you become convinced that your Russian is far from ideal – and that's it.

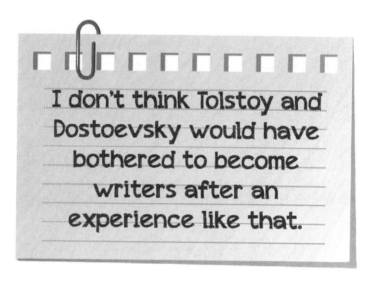

I don't think Tolstoy and Dostoevsky would have bothered to become writers after an experience like that. In fact, they probably wouldn't even have wanted to write in Russian! So what about Xavier and the millions of other students who dream of writing like Tolstoy while going through endless boring written exercises?

Why even bother with written Russian? Let's skip it!

A lot of progressive language learning programs don't even include written exercises. They try to exclude writing where possible. They usually explain this away by saying that *"the most important thing is live language and communication"* or *"writing should be taught as a separate skill"* and other similar excuses.

The real reason that people are writing less and less is because it is really difficult to force an adult student to actually write anything. It's no surprise – if a student learned a language in traditional school, then for him/her there is nothing more boring than the written exercise part. The student spends hours writing, gets a load of dreaded red pen corrections and feels like he/she doesn't know anything.

So, really, what do we have to lose? Let's just skip it altogether!

Why and when should I write?

As it turns out, skipping the writing part can be tough. So first, I would like to remind you why, in actual fact, we *need* written Russian and why it has its rightful place in this book.

Let's think back to the language learning formula that I hope you spent plenty of time studying in the chapter *"The language learning formula: 7 simple steps"*. Allow me to remind you of the order in which we approach language study:

- First we master **the speech positions** and then **learn to pronounce** Russian sounds, syllables and words at a natural speed.

- We **listen and learn to 'flow'** with Russian speech at a natural pace. Russian speech stops sounding like a mess of incomprehensible sounds flowing faster than a waterfall.

- We **build our vocabulary** by reading and listening. We are ready for this because we spent time learning to properly hear and pronounce Russian words and phrases.

- We **get acquainted with grammar** forms. We don't just sit there and learn 300 rules from a grammar textbook – we learn them as we go.

- Finally, we decide we want to speak Russian and **sound natural** – and not like some Google Translate robot. It's here, at this stage, that written Russian can help us achieve this goal.

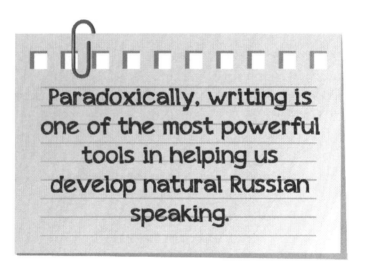

Paradoxically, writing is one of the most powerful tools in helping us develop natural Russian speaking.

Paradoxically, writing is one of the most powerful tools in helping us develop natural Russian *speaking*. At a zero-stress pace, we can express all of our Russian thoughts. We can get our work corrected by a native speaker. And, unlike in a conversation, we won't be interrupted mid-phrase with corrections. The best part is, we can keep our corrected text and make use of it later on in our studies.

Now you will know *exactly* when to start perfecting your written Russian. And you'll also know exactly *why you should be writing* too. Just writing on its own is not our goal. Although we used some of the Russian greats as examples, we don't want to become novelists. Written Russian is a tool and the end goal is natural, grammatically correct Russian.

As you can see, written Russian is a powerful 'weapon'. The key is to use it correctly and not the way most students do…

How we 'fixed' Xavier

Do you remember what Xavier's problem was? He was complaining that his Russian wasn't 'beautiful'! What kind of problem is that? Proper case usage, sure that's a *big* problem. Or Russian verbs of motion, another serious stumbling block… But language 'beauty'?

Sure, Xavier wasn't upset that his Russian was worse than the classic Russian writers'. He was disappointed because, even knowing so many words and grammar rules, he still didn't know how to use them and sound natural like a Russian native speaker. And this can lead to misunderstanding and getting totally lost in translation.

What came to the rescue was written exercises! We did all kinds of written exercises, but in a way such that they stopped feeling like a punishment and started to 'beautify' his Russian!

Step one: there is no fixed topic or volume

In step one, I didn't set Xavier any topics. Maybe he didn't want to write an essay on 'complaints in a restaurant' because he *didn't have any complaints!* (If he did have some complaints, then he could write an essay on that topic if he wanted to.) For example, he was getting ready to go on a trip around Russia's Golden Ring (a ring of historic cities around Moscow) and wrote a letter with questions on hotel booking to make sure he had all the information he needed.

This was something he thought of, but you can think up anything you find relevant or interesting.

The amount of words wasn't important either – nobody is going to tell an adult how many words he can write or say to express himself. I personally feel quite stupid when I have to write some fixed amount of words. What if I already said enough? What if I'm just filling a text with 'fluff'? This is exactly why our first step was to choose free-from writing that made sense to the student.

Step two: rewrite

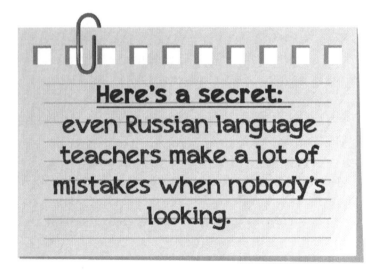

Here's a secret: even Russian language teachers make a lot of mistakes when nobody's looking.

Even though Xavier's grammar was good, he still made mistakes when writing an essay. Don't worry about it too much! Here's a secret: even Russian language teachers make a lot of mistakes when nobody's looking.

Our focus wasn't on grammar mistakes. The thing that sets apart native speech from foreign speech is how 'natural' it sounds. When you have a thought, you simply 'pull' a ready-made common phrase from your memory. As a rule, it's precisely these types of standard structures that language learners lack.

We need step two. It's not correcting, but *rewriting* – rewording your own thoughts in a form familiar to Russian speakers. Naturally we need to correct the grammar mistakes too, but they are not the main focus. We all make mistakes!

The end result was that Xavier received his small text, totally rewritten in natural sounding Russian.

And why did he need this text?

Step three: the most important part – making it stick

Xavier simply took the rewritten text and read it. Then he tried reading it out loud, many times. After all, these were his thoughts and ideas, expressed in normal, correct Russian. This wasn't some essay about a distant topic with corrected mistakes. This text is something he could show his friends with pride and reread later himself – because the text had value for him.

Best of all, Xavier set up a system for repetition (and you should too).

Put your text in a prominent spot and come back to it at roughly these intervals:

- after few hours

- after a day

- after 2-3 days

- after a week

- after a few more weeks to a month

Having a schedule is great, but you shouldn't spend too much time analysing the intervals. Just the act of revisiting the text to refresh your memory is great!

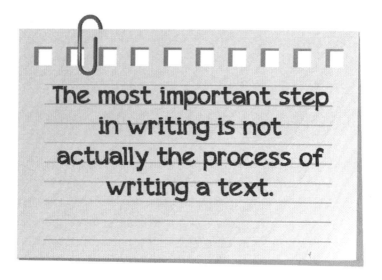

The most important step in writing is not actually the process of writing a text.

The most important step in writing is not actually the process of writing a text. It is the part where you absorb your own thoughts in natural-sounding Russian. If you miss this step, you've wasted your time.

How it helped Xavier and how it can help you too

Without a doubt, the process of writing-rewriting-repetition is much more fun and interesting than the average, boring written exercises. This is already half the battle. It won't hurt your motivation.

What effect will this have on the level and quality of your Russian?

Firstly, when writing, you are thinking things over, carefully choosing your words and phrases. You express yourself as correctly as possible. Your written text will probably be more complex and grammatically correct than oral speech.

Then you will get a rewritten and corrected text, and this has a powerful psychological effect. Your own thoughts, in different words – but they are still your thoughts! This is something you will pay much more attention to than just a grammar-corrected text – it's human nature.

You're basically creating your own study texts.

Isn't it amazing to study Russian using a mini-textbook that you created yourself?

This type of writing can help you really make a breakthrough.

This is quite often the last piece of the puzzle to push your Russian to the next level.

Enough of the theory: here is your assignment

If your level of Russian is good enough, I encourage you to start writing something today, and even better, right now!

Pick your topic

This is real life – your life – so your topic can range from sending texts to scientific articles. If you keep a diary, could you write a summary entry about today? Maybe there is something you could blog about? Maybe you want to write a note to somebody? Want to write an email to your boss asking for a raise? Just remember, it doesn't have to be a complex text! If you are a beginner, it could just be a to-do list or even a shopping list.

Really get creative and don't bother writing anything that isn't somehow relevant for you!

Get writing

It doesn't matter how basic the Russian is. Maybe you only know a few words right now. Or maybe you are at a level where you can publish an article in a Russian scientific journal. Try to avoid grammar mistakes where possible, but don't worry about it if you do make errors. After all, the text will be rewritten.

Get your rewritten text

Get your text back in natural Russian. You don't have to spend time and money seeking out fancy highly-qualified certified

Russian teachers. Any average Russian native speaker can help you. Of course, your selected native should be literate enough to be able to give your texts a check. The main thing to explain to your chosen native speaker is that they *shouldn't just correct your texts*. You need your text to be rewritten *in natural Russian*.

Read and recite

If you really want to get the most out of your experience, create an 'environment of repetition'. An actual environment, not just a fixed time where you sit down and do it. An example of an environment is when the text is jumping out at you from all angles, literally screaming 'read me again'. This could be a sticky note on your desk or a note in your planner. Whatever works best for you! If you really wrote your text from the heart, then your rewritten version should be a pleasure to read!

Secret time: how to get the most out of writing

I'm sure after writing something according to this new method, you will feel the difference. It's so far away from the boring and dull writing that may have tortured you before!

Here I want to remind you one more time: we are not just writing in Russian for the sake of writing. Sure, that might be useful if you want to be a journalist or pass a Russian test. But our 'secret' goal is to teach you to express your thoughts in natural Russian – both in writing and orally.

Now let's make sure you use your time properly:

- Avoid 'artificial' writing exercises (like 'insert the missing word'). Writing is a natural and everyday task.

- If you feel it's too early for you to start writing in Russian and think it's too hard, don't worry – this is normal. Writing isn't easy, and it comes after listening and reading.

- Forcing an adult to write a set amount of words on some boring topic is not natural. Only write about things that are relevant and interesting to you.

- Speaking Russian naturally, like a native speaker, is more important than being 100% grammatically correct. Instead of just getting some routine grammar mistakes corrected, you need the rewrite of your thoughts in natural Russian.

- The most useful thing about writing is not the actual writing process – it's the repetition of natural and correct Russian. Your rewritten text is better than any Russian study guide. Just make sure you read and repeat it.

And finally, here's an important question: how long do you need to do this writing for? What result can you expect?

My answer is always the same: do it for as long as you're learning the language. Get into the habit of always doing some writing once a week, even if it's just a little essay. This will train and 'condition' your brain to express thoughts and ideas clearly and correctly.

7 Practical Steps – Take Action Today

If you were to read only one chapter in this whole book, do you know which one I would recommend?

I would recommend this one right here!

First off, it's the shortest – for those short on time. Secondly, it's all about practise – for those who like more action, less talk and more results.

So, if you have skipped the whole book and come straight here, that's OK. You can always go back to the other chapters later.

Back to why we're here. You have decided to start and want to know which step to start with. Start with step one and you won't go far wrong. If you feel you have that skill under control, move on to the next step.

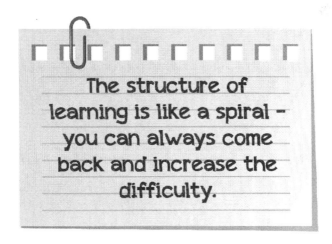

The structure of learning is like a spiral – you can always come back and increase the difficulty.

The structure of learning is like a spiral – you can always come back and increase the difficulty.

1. Learn the speech positions and 'unfriendly' Russian sounds

Even when just starting a language, you need some phonetics. Before jumping into listening, vocab building and learning the alphabet, you need to know about Russian sounds and pronunciation.

This step is really important as you need to know how the sounds of your native language differ from Russian. You don't want to be pronouncing Russian using sounds from your own language!

You can find out more about sounds and speech position in *Chapter 1. Pronunciation can ruin everything*. The key points are:

- Identifying Russian sounds that aren't in your native language. I call these your 'obvious enemies' – they are few and they are easy to spot.

- Don't miss mini-lesson 7 on the most 'unfriendly' sounds.

- Sounds that both your native tongue and Russian have can be tricky. I call these the 'hidden' enemies. To avoid speaking Russian with a funny accent, you need to master the Russian speech positions. Your speech muscles need to adopt a special position (like a stance in sports). This will take time and it's something you will need to practise.

At this step, right at the start, you will learn to correctly pronounce Russian sounds and get your speech muscles performing the proper movements. This won't get rid of your accent right away, but it will give you a chance to practise and improve.

2. Learn to speak at natural speed – Repetition lesson

The skill of fluent speech is the foundation. This is the basis for all the other skills. By mastering the ability to quickly pronounce sentences, you'll be set for success for the rest of your learning.

Remember, if you speak Russian slowly and make mistakes, the Repetition lesson is for you. Find out more in *Chapter 1. Pronunciation can ruin everything.* Here's what the repetition process looks like:

1. Listen to a short audio a few times and try to understand it.

2. Read a text. Translate it if necessary.

3. Start with syllables, **repeating small sections**, then move on to longer phrases. Lots of repetition – out loud!

4. **Read some sentences** or a paragraph with correct pronunciation **at a normal speed** – 120 words per minute.

5. **Now speed up** –try to read small texts out loud at 200 words per minute.

Start right away! Book readers can find a video Repetition lesson in the Bonus section of www.learningrussianmarathonbook.com.

The Repetition lesson will teach your speech muscles to make the correct movements at a normal speed. You will become more confident. Fast-spoken Russian speech will start to sound less scary!

3. Flowing with Russian speech – Vocal Listening

For anyone who really has problems with listening comprehension, pay close attention.

You can learn more about beating your difficulties in *Chapter 3. Don't understand Russian? Just smile and nod!*

This is the exercise where you will learn to listen actively, not passively. Here's a breakdown of the Vocal Listening lesson:

1. Spend a few minutes **listening to audio with no text**. You will try to silently repeat the sounds, syllables, and words along with the audio track.

2. We break down the text and translate it, if needed. We listen, follow along with the text and **read it out loud along with the recording**.

3. We set the text aside and **listen again, repeating simultaneously** – loudly and out loud.

The main thing here is, when reading along out loud, you don't have to wait – you can speak along with the audio, perhaps lagging a few words behind.

You can do this on your own and for free! You don't need a teacher and you don't need a special audio course. All you need is a podcast with some text.

Your speech apparatus will get used to working at Russian native level. Vocal Listening will teach you to listen carefully and understand Russian at normal speed.

4. Building your vocabulary – Reading

Even with a fantastic memory, learning all the forms of Russian words is hard. What's even harder is using them correctly afterward!

This step is for you if you have a small vocab right now or have trouble using words properly.

The method is laid out in *Chapter 4. Memory like a super computer?*

Here's what you'll be doing:

1. Find a Russian text that fits your level – you should find several new words per page.

2. **Read the text**, and preferably listen to it too.

3. If you guess a new word based on context, **highlight it and the whole phrase** in the text (you don't need to use a dictionary or write things out on a separate sheet).

4. Make sure you **repeat the highlighted phrases** and words. Skim the text and recall them. Set up a repetition system for yourself. For example: after 5 minutes, 30 minutes, 2-3 hours, a few days, 1 week, 3 weeks.

The result will be that you build your vocab without having to study lists of words. You won't be learning individual words from the dictionary, but actual constructs (phrases) in context. This is a much easier and more effective way of memorising.

5. Internalise grammar forms – Grammar Variation

Learn how to 'feel' Russian grammar. You should feel and know instinctively what sounds correct in Russian and what doesn't.

This step will be perfect for you if you know Russian grammar rules but still make mistakes when speaking because you can't keep up and have to stop and think all the time about which grammar rule you need.

You'll learn all about the hardships and 'secrets' of Russian grammar in *Chapter 5. Grammar every day.*

Here is how you will master Russian grammar without killing yourself with case tables, rules and exceptions:

1. Take a small text in Russian – a story. Pay close attention as you listen to the story and read it. Translate the parts you don't understand.

2. Listen to this story from another perspective (if it was first person, switch to third person, etc.)

3. Change the tense – listen to the story in the future, past and present tense.

4. Listen to the story told in the imperative.

No suitable audio for Grammar Variations? Don't worry, I have you covered! Your Grammar Variation lesson is in the Bonus section of www.learningrussianmarathonbook.com. Don't put it off another minute – start right away!

By listening to grammar forms change in live context and different tenses, you will learn to 'feel' grammar. This method won't overload your brain and won't make you lose your confidence.

6. Write and sound natural – "Write – Rewrite – Review"

You'll learn to express your thoughts in correct, natural Russian, both verbally and orally. You will be using written exercises the effective way – *not the way they're usually taught in class*. If you still sound unnatural and often incorrect in Russian, these written exercises could be what you need.

Here's what the write, rewrite, review system looks like:

1. You think about **a topic you want to write about**. No boring topics, only things you find interesting!

2. **Write it!** Any type of text and any length.

3. Ask a native speaker (it doesn't have to be a teacher) to **rewrite your text**, making it sound like natural Russian.

4. **Repeat and review** the corrected text many times – your thoughts, but expressed in natural Russian.

You will learn just why writing is so important in *Chapter 6. Why you hate writing Russian.*

By using the *"Write – Rewrite – Review"* method, you are basically creating your own textbook. This has a powerful psychological effect! Seeing your texts and thoughts in correct natural Russian will help it stay in your memory.

7. Hold a conversation – Storytelling lesson

It doesn't matter what your Russian level is, you can always start to speak freely. For most people, speaking in Russian is stressful, but by sitting there in silence, listening, you'll never learn to hold a conversation.

Storytelling lessons will be perfect for you if you speak Russian slowly, with pauses. Perhaps you know you need speaking practise, but you find it stressful and unpleasant.

The most powerful technique for learning to speak Russian with ease is laid out in *Chapter 2. Fluent autopilot Russian – dreams come true*. In short, here's what a storytelling lesson looks like:

1. The teacher reads a simple phrase that you understand. You **listen** and maybe nod along.

2. **The teacher asks lots and lots of simple questions** based on what you just listened to.

3. You have to **answer every question quickly**, out loud and, preferably, loudly.

4. You repeat the lesson over and over again. The goal is to get used to answering quickly and automatically.

If you find it hard to imagine this in action, have a look now. Come and check out the Storytelling video lesson in the Bonus section of www.learningrussianmarathonbook.com.

Lots of storytelling repetition is what will help you become 'automatic' when answering. You will learn to give simple answers without thinking, pausing or stuttering. Your fear of speaking will eventually disappear.

***

You know, I am worried that, having read all the chapters, you will put off taking action on the advice to some later time. That's the way people are – we subconsciously try to find reasons *not to do* something here and now – even if we know it will help us.

Changing our approach and trying new things is hard for us. Which of these resonates the most with you?

"It's too hard..."

"I don't see the point in doing that..."

"I'm not sure that I'll see the benefits..."

"I don't have something to get started with now..."

I hope that, logically, you understand that these are all fairly weak excuses. When writing this book I wanted to be practical.

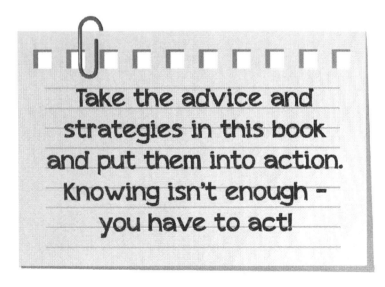

Take the advice and strategies in this book and put them into action. Knowing isn't enough – you have to act!

Take the advice and strategies in this book and put them into action.

Knowing isn't enough – you have to act!

Of course, I'm not so naive to think you will put absolutely all the advice in the book into action. However, I am sure that you are a mature, thoughtful reader. So I believe you will take the best elements of this book and change your approach to learning Russian dramatically!

Afterword

The story continues…

I would like to believe that one day, in the near future, we shall see a scientific breakthrough that makes learning foreign languages easy and painless. Much like the invention of the camera made it possible to capture images in an instant, without having to study painting.

Sadly, it would seem that things are different with languages. I don't think we'll get to enjoy such a breakthrough in our lifetimes. For the moment, the path of a polyglot is one paved with hardships.

But you can take solace in the face that many language learners eventually conquer their difficulties and achieve their desired results – if in no language other than their native tongue.

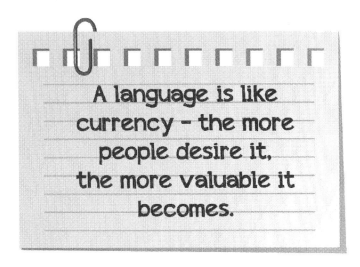

A language is like
currency – the more
people desire it,
the more valuable it
becomes.

It reminds me of a thought I once had on my way home: a language is like currency – the more people desire it, the more valuable it becomes. And much like currency, language can be widespread, but if people fail to see value in it, the result is devaluation.

Some time ago I felt there was a similar devaluation happening to the Russian language. Without people seeing value in Russian, the language's legacy, centuries of work, will be reduced to nothing more than piles of meaningless paper.

Your interest in Russian imparts certain energy. It increases the value of the language.

So it's not so important that you master Russian to a Tolstoy and Dostoevsky level, or you might only know the alphabet. What is important is your interest. It is your interest that keeps Russian 'alive'.

Knowing Russian is not just a matter a knowing words or correct grammar. It's a lot more than that. By learning Russian…

…we can touch the past and experience the history created by Russian speakers.

…we can understand the Russian mentality.

…we save the language as a cultural legacy, passing it along to future generations.

By learning Russian, we can all play a small role in the ongoing history of the language!

Printed in Poland
by Amazon Fulfillment
Poland Sp. z o.o., Wrocław

28938145R00090